The God Who Created Us

Printed in the United States of America
ISBN: Softcover   978-1-969213-29-8
              e-Book   978-1-969213-30-4
Republished by: TwinVerse Prime
Publication Date: 10/20/2025

To order copies of this book, contact:
TwinVerse Prime
Phone: (725) 257-6538
clients@twinverseprime.com
www.twinverseprime.com/

CONTENTS

ACKNOWLEDGEMENTS

To the God who has inspired me to write on His word

Ramon who designed the cover

DEDICATION

To the Lord my God who trained me
to write and interpret scripture

BOOKS PUBLISHED BY PETER

Biblical Comment:
The Origin of Life : God's Relationship with Man in Genesis
God Rescues His People : Birth of Nation According to Exodus
The Wilderness Training School : Powerful Lessons in Numbers
Seeing Into the Future : Understanding the Revelation of John
The Path of Wisdom : A Study of Proverbs Chapters 1 to 4
Proverbs 5 to 12
Hosea
Deuteronomy
Epistle to the Ephesians
Epistle to the Colossians
Epistle to the Romans
Epistle to the Hebrews
Epistle to the Galatians

Matters of Faith:
Are There Demons? & Other Matters of Faith
Letters to the Seven Churches in Revelation
Lost Souls : The danger of losing sight of God
Covenant & Testament : God's rules for God's people to obey
Belief and Faith : Understanding the Essentials
Ordinary People : Extra-ordinary faith
So You Think You Know About Faith : Learning to Trust God
A Fresh Look at Easter
You Will Receive Power
Assuredly God IS!
Truth & Doubt
Christ IS King : A Guide for Doubters
Law & Grace (Lessons from the Kings of Judah & Israel)
The God Who created Us

Autobiographical:
A Tale of Three Men (Provides background information about how these books came to be written and distributed)

What our faith is all about
The Tent of the Meeting : Illustrating God's Plan of Salvation

INTRODUCTION

If we do not know who God is, how can we worship Him, or even get to know Him in any meaningful way?

It is in our created nature to want to worship something much bigger than ourselves, to understand the purpose of our life here on this earth, so it is in our own interests for us discover for ourselves just who God is and how we should relate to Him.

For Christians the basis of our search for any knowledge of God must be concentrated in the Bible. Indeed, the whole purpose of this book is just that. Searching through the Bible to give us the best and simplest understanding of the God who created us so that we can properly worship Him and, most important of all, relate to Him and serve Him.

Throughout my life I have been intrigued with God, indeed He has increasingly become central to my life so that I now have a passion to pass on all that I have discovered about Him to others.

1 WHO IS GOD?

God is a Spirit

The first four words of Genesis tells us that *In the beginning God ...* In order to discover as much as we can about The God Who Created Us, that must be our starting point.

What those first four words tell us is that before anything was made that was made God existed. Without the existence of anything physical, it is logical to conclude that God is Spirit, that is:

- He was never born and will never die,
- He is without a form that the human eye could see or even imagine,
- He inhabits a completely vacant space with no beginning or ending, no height, nor depth, nor width.

How can we possibly grasp the magnitude of such a concept? Endless space filled by One who is also *omnipresent* and a thinking, reasoning person in their own right with feelings and sensitivity.

Therefore we cannot call God 'it' because He is a person with character; one who possess all the attributes He gave to man and much more for He is way above us and beyond us in every aspect of His being.

He is also *omniscient*, which means there is nothing whatsoever that He does not know or indeed is capable of doing, because he alone knows the means by which an end can be achieved with the ability to do it. Not even the contents of all the knowledge collectively held by all the libraries in the world could possibly match His wisdom, knowledge and understanding. In fact it could all be thrown away as useless. As we will discover later on, man is very restricted in His thinking, whereas God is not.

> 13 *Who has directed the Spirit of the Lord,*
> *Or as His counselor has taught Him?*
> 14 *With whom did He take counsel, and who instructed Him,*
> *And taught Him in the path of justice?*
> *Who taught Him knowledge,*
> *And showed Him the way of understanding?*
> (Is. 40)

> 34 *"For who has known the mind of the Lord?*
> *Or who has become His counselor?"*
> 35 *"Or who has first given to Him*
> *And it shall be repaid to him?"*
> 36 *For of Him and through Him*
> *and to Him are all things,*
> *to whom be glory forever. Amen.*
> (Ro. 11)

Every non-fiction subject that is relevant to our life on this earth started with Him. All the sciences emanated from the creation which He initiated and completed to His satisfaction. Many of the early scientists who discovered how things of the earth and the universe worked initially established the sciences, from which they grew to be major subjects of research. But not one individual is capable of knowing all there is to know, in fact man is still discovering new things and recording them but having to specialize more and more as the store of information grows.

Added to that He is *omnipotent*. All power that has existed from time immemorial resides in Him, because in the very beginning there was no other being, other than God, no not one. That means the whole of creation from the greatest mountain to the minutest microbe was designed and brought into being solely through His limitless ability and resources. Because He alone was responsible for the whole physical creation coming into being, He alone must also sustain it without any reduction of His power and authority for there is no one but Him outside of creation. He created all things and therefore sustains all things and will one day cause it all to disappear into nothing just as it appeared in the first place out of nothing.

If we cannot grasp the magnitude of God from that, then there is something wrong with us.

...God created the heavens and the earth.

No one can say all that is physical was not created because even the evolutionists tell us that in the beginning there was a big bang and both the material that exploded and what caused it to explode had logically to be provided and caused by someone.

That is the major flaw in the theory of Evolution. Who caused it to happen and who caused it to end up being the incredibly complex physical wonder that it is, is not included in the theory of evolution.

In the book of Revelation chapter 4:11 we read this:

"You are worthy, O Lord,
To receive glory and honor and power;
For You created all things.
By Your will they were created
and continue to exist."

The whole principle underlying the creation is truth. But truth is positive and man has erred from the truth with many lies abounding. When Adam sinned all the positivity with which God had created the world and the universe was set aside in the minds of men.

Just consider two aspects of the creation that will highlight this matter.

Light is positive, darkness is negative. Think about a very dark night, completely devoid of light of any kind, just impenetrable blackness such that it wraps you tightly in its grip. The very moment a candle is lit, however small, what happens to the darkness? Which predominates, the darkness or the light of the candle?

We all know that the positive nature of light overcomes the negative darkness. What does the Bible say about this? *God is light and in Him is no darkness at all, but men prefer the darkness rather than light for their deeds are evil.*

Let us consider another aspect of positive and negative.

Love is positive for it binds people together and happiness abounds, whereas hatred is negative for it divides and separates. There could be no love in the world except it came from God, for

He is the ultimate source of all things, whereas hatred was born when Adam sinned and Satan gained control of the world.

Later we will have to consider the complexity of God, but in the meantime let us continue with considering the first verse of the Bible for there is much that it can reveal to us.

The earth was without form, and void;
and darkness was on the face of the deep.

The Bible tells us that the creation did not happen in an instant, therefore some credit must be given to the evolutionists who through years of research discovered this fact. However, their failure is to be unable to go back to before the big bang and identify the One behind the big bang!

Obviously after the big bang, fragments of the exploding material were distributed throughout this endless space. But here we have another conundrum. For God to have His space there needed to be some containment of the creational material. After all although God is the author of creation He is not part of it, therefore He has to remain outside creation whilst having access to it.

The reason why He needs to keep Himself separate is the contrast between His purity and our fallen state.

When God created man and put him in the garden man was able to talk to God face to face, for God was able to make Himself seen by man. Also man was not only pure, having just been created by God, but God also breathed His Spirit into man creating a spirit within him that allowed him to communicate directly with God. At that time all in the garden was totally pure.

We speak about man speaking with God in the Garden, but which member of the Godhead? The one part of the trinity who consistently came to the earth, in the beginning to meet with Adam, was the Son who is the only member of the trinity who has been directly associated with man from the beginning, as we shall discover in a later chapter.

As soon as man sinned he was condemned to enter into a relationship with God that was indirect, because God could not look upon sin or deal directly with those who had sinned but not been cleansed of that sin.

This was particularly significant when the Son of God was

5

hanging on the cross, dying in our place for our sins, because that was the only time the Father had to turn His face away from His Son. No wonder Jesus cried out, *My God, My God, why have you forsaken Me?*

We refer to God being in His heaven and in Hebrews we read that all those who rebel against God, indeed all those that have no time for God no matter whether or not it is an active or inactive rebellion, will not enter into His rest (Hb. 4:7 – 15), that is they will not be allowed into His space outside of creation after their physical death, and after judgement before the great white throne when the saved and unsaved will be separated.

When Moses asked to see God, he was told *"You cannot see My face; for no man shall see Me, and live."* He was only allowed to see His back. But His face would have shone with such purity that Moses would have died from the shock of seeing total purity compared to his sinfulness.

It is significant that whenever Moses had been with God His face shone with the reflected glory of God. The skin of his face absorbed the glory surrounding the person of God and caused his face to shine for a while before it faded. But the brightness of that fading glory was such that the rebellious Israelites asked him to put a veil over his face after he had passed on God's message to them.

Isaiah wrote that he saw the Lord high and lifted up with seraphim calling out *Holy, holy , holy is the Lord of hosts, the whole earth is full of His glory.* This prompted the priest Isaiah to cry out:

> *"Woe is me, for I am undone!*
> *Because I am a man of unclean lips,*
> *And I dwell in the midst of a people of unclean lips;*
> *For my eyes have seen the King,*
> *The Lord of hosts."*

The antidote given to him by God was for one of the seraphim to touch Isaiah's lips with a live coal from the altar for purification.

Daniel (7:9, 10) was allowed to see into heaven:

> *I watched till thrones were put in place,*
> *And the Ancient of Days was seated;*
> *His garment was white as snow,*
> *And the hair of His head was like pure wool.*

His throne was a fiery flame,
Its wheels a burning fire;
A fiery stream issued
And came forth from before Him.
A thousand thousands ministered to Him;
Ten thousand times ten thousand stood before Him.

The apostle John was invited into heaven to be shown things that were to take place in the future, and there he saw a throne set in heaven (Rev. 4:1 – 5).

So how do we account for the creation and the heaven which is God's place of rest? Having considered this matter for many years the only way I can understand it is by thinking of a great big bubble within endless space into which God fitted His creation. It is impossible for man to get to the edge of the bubble as there is so much of the universe and the time for man to get from one near planet is long enough; to try and get to another galaxy would take more than a lifetime, and the inability to store enough food and oxygen makes the journey impossible.

Also there is a problem with the longevity of the earth. God made it a place of testing the loyalty of man towards Him, after all He placed two trees in the centre of the garden into which he placed the first man and woman with the eating of the fruit of just one being forbidden. The test of man resulted in failure which caused man to be evicted from the garden to fend for himself rather than being supplied from the plants in the garden.

So rather than having everything supplied along with regular meetings in the cool of the day with his maker, man had to scratch a living from the soil, with the woman having pain in childbirth.

It seems to me that as the area of earth's surface is fixed and as God instructed man to multiply and fill the earth, knowing full well that when man started to use all the resources God had made available to him, not only would man find that as he multiplied there would be less and less spare room for him, animals and an area for growing food, but harmful gasses would be released that would cause the earth to deteriorate not only with regard to the environment, but as man separated himself from God just as Cain did, he would also gradually destroy his habitat, which is what is happening right now.

By separating the whole of creation into a bubble, God was able to determine all that was going on within it and get involved with man as required until the moment when He had already planned for the life of the earth to come to an end when all that was in the bubble would be all burned up and disappear.

God is three

Now let us continue our journey of discovering what we can of God, but doing so is not that easy for in our finite minds how can one God in fact be three individuals? The first four words clearly states that *In the beginning God ...*, with God being singular. We have concluded that God is singular because only one is mentioned and we also have to assume that as nothing physical had been created *In the beginning ...*, God had to be a Spirit, that is a person without a physical body.

However, in verse 2 we are told that *the Spirit of God*, not the Spirit that was God, *was hovering over the face of the waters.*

What is interesting about that is, from where did the water come? The one thing that can be said about the Bible's account of the creation is that it is not a step by step narrative. Some rock substance exploded because at their core all the planets are rock.

So if all that was flung into the space within the bubble at the beginning were fragments of rock, from where did the water come? What is more, water can only lay in recesses on the surface of a rock, so how did the rock change shape to provide depressions on the surface in which the water could collect?

From fragments (plural) of rock, blown into space, the Bible now focuses on the earth.

Apart from the one God being Spirit, we now discover that there is a Spirit of God who *was hovering over the face of the waters,* which means the senior figure is still outside the bubble.

Before we proceed any further it is important that we discover the secret about the members of the one God and their place within the Godhead:

Father, who has never left His place of rest is the controlling part of God.

Son, also known as the Word of God, who visited the earth at least twice before he was born in human flesh. He spoke what the Father was thinking. He is the mouthpiece.

Spirit, referred to as the Holy Spirit or the Spirit of God, has been at work in the world since Genesis 1:1.

What can we discover about the Spirit who was *hovering over the face of the waters?* A great deal because the Spirit of God is what might be call the Spirit of action for it was the spirit who caused things to happen, for the creation to become a reality and for what the Lord said when He was on the earth as a man to happen such as raising the dead, stilling the storm, casting out demons, telling the Son what people in His vicinity were thinking and much more.

It was also He who spoke the words of the Son to the prophets of old and even in the present day.

> *However, when He, the Spirit of truth, has come, He will guide you into all truth; for He will not speak on His own authority, but whatever He hears He will speak; and He will tell you things to come.*

The things of God are hidden from all men, except those who are open to the voice of God. And, because the Godhead cannot be separated, the Spirit was with the Lord during His time on the earth. Consider two verses in Luke 10:21, 22)

> *In that hour Jesus rejoiced in the Spirit and said, "I thank You, Father, Lord of heaven and earth, that You have hidden these things from the wise and prudent and revealed them to babes. Even so, Father, for so it seemed good in Your sight.*

The Father to Son relationship is here made very clear, for the Son refers to His Father as the Lord of heaven and earth. In John's gospel Jesus clearly states that He had come to do the will of His Father. Thus we have a hierarchical structure of the Father and the Son, a relationship that will never end because God is eternal. What is also most interesting is that the Son represents the Father and the Father represents the Son, for Jesus told the disciples that in seeing Him they had in effect seen the Father.

What was not said was that the Father did not have any form, but without the human body provided by Mary, which the Son used to visit the earth and be able to live amongst and speak to people, neither did the Son. What the people saw was a human body which was inhabited by the Spirit that was the Son of God. Moreover, the glory of God that would have put the lives of the disciples and those that met with Him at risk was attenuated by the body of the Lord.

The unique truth about the second of the two verses is that the whole of the Godhead, even when the Son was on the earth, worked in total unison, in a union that is unbreakable and unshakeable.

> *22 All things have been delivered to Me by My Father, and no*
> *one knows who the Son is except the Father, and who the Father is*
> *except the Son, and the one to whom the Son wills to reveal Him."*

Thus we could say that the Son is the voice of the Father and the information only flows from the Godhead to individuals as the Lord sees fit. But the Son does not know all that the Father knows, such as the timing of His second coming.

Which leads us to the Spirit. Notice that it is the Spirit who was *hovering over the face of the waters.* We could say that the Spirit wore the overalls. The Son spoke the words of the Father, and the Spirit caused things to happen.

This can be clearly illustrated when Jesus called for the wind to stop allowing the water in the Galilean Lake to become calm. It was not Jesus who caused the wind to stop, it was the Spirit of God in obedience to the command of the Son.

When Jesus knew what the religious leaders were thinking, it had nothing to do with a sixth sense, it was the Spirit of God telling the Lord what they were thinking, for it is the Spirit who can see even into the dark recesses of the heart of man[1]. Those opponents of the Lord did not realize that the Spirit was able to get inside them and know exactly what they were thinking, what was in their hearts; their attitude towards Him.

When the Lord was hanging on the cross, the Spirit of God was there as a witness to the shedding of the blood, for it is the Spirit who causes the blood to be efficacious:

> *14 how much more shall the blood of Christ, who through the*
> *eternal Spirit offered Himself without spot to God, cleanse your*
> *conscience from dead works to serve the living God? (Heb. 9)*

---

[1] To Hebrew thought the heart as mentioned is not the physical heart but the centre of a person, their inner being from which thoughts and feelings stem.

It is not possible to separate the three members of the Godhead, even though in the New Testament they can clearly be seen performing completely different but supportive roles. Today, with the Son back with the Father, it is the Spirit of God who is the only member of the Godhead fully at work on the earth. For as John recorded (Jn. 16):

> 7 *Nevertheless I tell you the truth. It is to your advantage that I go away; for if I do not go away, the Helper will not come to you; but if I depart, I will send Him to you.*
>
> 8 *And when He has come, He will convict the world of sin, and of righteousness, and of judgment:*
>
> 9 *of sin, because they do not believe in Me;*
>
> 10 *of righteousness, because I go to My Father and you see Me no more;*
>
> 11 *of judgment, because the ruler of this world is judged.*
>
> 12 *'I still have many things to say to you, but you cannot bear them now.*
>
> 13 *However, when He, the Spirit of truth, has come, He will guide you into all truth; for He will not speak on His own authority, but whatever He hears He will speak; and He will tell you things to come.*
>
> 14 *He will glorify Me, for He will take of what is Mine and declare it to you.*

Much is made about God only having to speak the word and it was done. In the Psalms we read *By the word of the Lord the heavens were made, And all the host of them by the breath of His mouth. (33:6)* and that is true because the Spirit only does what God the Father says through the Son, just as the Son only speaks the words of His Father. But each one is nothing without the other two. The authority is in the total Godhead.

There is one more question that needs answering and that is how did Genesis come to be written when no one was alive until Adam appeared on the earth and the ability to record events was not available until a long time after Adam had died? Clearly it was the Holy Spirit speaking to Moses, the supposed author of the first five books of he Bible.

Throughout this book we will gradually learn more about our remarkable God

2 MAN

The Image of God

Then God said, "Let Us make man in Our image, according to Our likeness; let them have dominion over the fish of the sea, the birds of the air, the cattle, all the earth and over every creeping thing that creeps on the earth."

So God created man in His own image; in the image of God He created him; both male and female He created them.

Then God blessed them, and God said to them, "Be fruitful and multiply; fill the earth and subdue it; have dominion over the fish of the sea, over the birds of the air, and over every living thing that moves on the earth."

We now need to understand the awesomeness of God from the perspective of His design of man who was created in His image.

Nowhere in scripture is an explanation given as to why God wanted to create the heavens and the earth. All we have is that God said *"Let there be …"* and it appeared to His satisfaction. Such was His careful progressive work in creating the heavens and the earth and all that was on the earth that it takes up 25 verses of chapter 1 and causes the earth to take the center stage of his creation.

After the earth and all living beings and plants were created and living, and given the ability to multiply, God then decided to create man in His own image to oversee the earth that had been created separately to all other planets within the whole unique and vast solar system containing many galaxies.

Surely such vastness, and the fact that the earth is just one planet that orbits the sun, emphasizes to man just how great is God, and beyond understanding.

Let us first consider man as the apex of God's creation and from that seek to understand how he can be described as being in the image of God.

God created man from the dust of the ground, but he is not just a body but a complex being.

> *And the Lord God formed man of the dust of the ground, and breathed into his nostrils the breath of life; and man became a living being. (Gen. 2:7)*

Realizing that God took 15.75 billion years to compete the creation process before He rested from His labours, the formation of man from the dust of the ground, the only substance available, occurred in the last 0.25 billion years. It therefore took God, with great care and attention, some time from creating the first being to the point where man was elevated from just a member of the animal kingdom to being in charge of God's earthly creation.

Only the Torah (the first five books of Moses), and in particular the book of Genesis, gives a detailed explanation of each stage of the creation. This is from a leaflet written by the Jewish scientist Gerald Schroeder[2]:

- The first of the Biblical days lasted 24 hours, viewed from the "beginning of time perspective." But the duration from our perspective was 8 billion years.

- The second day, from the Bible's perspective lasted 24 hours. From our perspective it lasted half of the previous day, 4 billion years.

- The third day also lasted half of the previous day, 2 billion years.

- The fourth day - one billion years.

---

[2] See my book The Tent of the Meeting : Illustrating God's Plan of Salvation Appendix B

- The fifth day - one-half billion years.

- The sixth day - one-quarter billion years.

When you add up the Six Days, you get the age of the universe at 15 and 3/4 billion years; the same as modern cosmology. Is it by chance?

What is interesting is that all the Genesis text tells us is that *the Lord God formed man of the dust of the ground*. It does not give us any details of the method He used to produce the first man, therefore we are reliant on what man has discovered through carefully investigating and assessing all the evidence that has literally been unearthed over the years. The earth giving up its secrets.

What the statement *"the Lord God formed man of the dust of the ground,"* tells us is that all God had to start with was this fragment of material that exploded at the start of the creation process from which He produced all that we see around us, including all living beings except man.

When creating man on the sixth day God did not start from the beginning but took the male of a species He had already created and developed it separately to be able to stand upright and think for itself.

However much we might consider the failures of man, it is essential that we consider the product of God's creational skills at the beginning when everything was still perfect. It is said that we are descended from apes which to my mind has an element of truth because of all the archeological evidence that has been unearthed, collected and analyzed over centuries.

We must be careful not to go through the argument that rocked the church many centuries ago, when it insisted the world was flat even though scientists had discovered the world was spherical, and that instead of the sun going round the earth, the earth actually went round the sun. The earth was not the primary planet in our solar system but one of several.

The court cases pitting creationist against evolutionist were a sad reflection of dogma over the deep study of the scriptures along with other study material which clearly shows that both are known to be partly correct. By joining the two seamlessly together it is possible to build a clearer picture of what happened in the beginning and a better understanding of what has happened since. It is very important to consider all the facts.

> Then God said, "Let Us make man in Our image, according to Our likeness; let them have dominion over the fish of the sea, over the birds of the air, and over the cattle, over all the earth and over every creeping thing that creeps on the earth (Gen. 1:26 – 28).

With all the research done by man through the centuries along with the clear comparative factual evidence, it is clear that God in His wisdom developed man over the final quarter billion years of the creation process. The final result was a soul living in an upright body with the brain capacity capable of taking charge of the world that God had created.

Unlike members of the animal kingdom, that are mostly governed by instinct, man has been given the ability to speak, to create and use language to convey thoughts and ideas, to think for himself, collect and compute information, make assessments, outwit predators, invent/create/build things, the ability to understand how to grow food and farm animals, hunt and outwit prey. In fact the man God created had to be able to control all aspects of animal life.

These are all elements of the image of God that He designed into the first man and subsequently the woman who was developed from the rib-bone of the man. We are not impersonal *its*, but have been created with intellect, emotions and will for we are able to perceive or feel things.

When we were created we had wisdom and a moral compass, with a sense of good and bad, what was right and what was wrong. So when Satan said to Eve that *God knows when you eat of the forbidden fruit your eyes will be open, and you will be like God knowing good and evil*, he was encouraging the investigative nature and greed element within us to think they were gaining more. But that *knowing good and evil* would be from the standpoint of evil for it required man to rebel against God and fail the test of loyalty to the God who created us.

It was also necessary for individual members of the human kind to work together and bond with each other emotionally and practically, as he had desired man would interact with Him, in order to create and organize communities, to be able to regulate communities. And live in families of a man and his female wife to produce children who would be brought up in a loving family unit because God is Love and love was to be central to the life of all men (which included wo-men). All of these things are clearly in the image of God, for God has all these attributes and more.

And the Lord God formed man
of the dust of the ground,
and breathed into his nostrils the breath of life;
and man became a living being.
(Gen. 2:7)

The one feature that took mankind above the level of the animal kingdom was the ability to communicate with God. In the garden we know that God spoke directly to Adam in the cool of the day and this was made possible because of yet another act of God which was to breathe the breath of His Spirit into man creating within him a spirit that enabled man's soul to communicate directly with God.

It was a very special spiritual connectivity that also brought with it eternal life, enjoyed by no other created creature. However only by man maintaining a close spiritual relationship with our spiritual creator God is a life of service possible leading to an eternity with the person of God.

As Jesus said to the Samaritan woman at the well,

the hour is coming, and now is, when true worshipers will worship the Father in spirit and truth; for the Father is seeking such to worship Him. **God is Spirit,** *and those who worship Him must worship in spirit and truth. (Jn. 4:23, 24)*

Reflecting the first subheading of the first chapter of this book the statement the Lord Jesus made - *God is Spirit* - clearly establishes that element within man that resulted from that breath of God. It is that spirit which is so essential to our worshipful relationship to God. And worship is a critical element in our relationship with our sovereign creator God. After all we are His creatures made in His image and, most important of all, created for His good pleasure which means God created us to be His companions upon whom He could lavish His love and care. We cannot possibly care for Him

17

except for the fact that it is He who cares for us.

Out of Tune with God

Cain was the first person to reject God outright which meant that without spiritual food the God breathed Spirit within him died of starvation, for the food that keeps alive the spirit within us is every word that proceeds from the mouth of God, (Matt. 4:4) because it is spiritual food from a Spiritual God.

To Nicodemus Jesus spoke of the need to be born again. It was very clear that the God breathed spirit within Nicodemus was no longer alive because, although he recognized that there was something special about the Lord, from a spiritual sense he did not recognize Him as Adam, in his pure initial state, would have done. Therefore the spirit within Nicodemus had to be re-born, regenerated, made alive again by the Spirit of God (Jn. 3:6).

God is and always will be the creator and sustainer of all that exists and although He delegated control over the earth to man, He never relinquished His ability to step in and take control should the need arise. For instance, from His place outside creation He still has the ability to shake the heavens and the earth, the sea and the dry land.

> *Then God said, "Let Us make man in Our image, according to Our likeness; let them have dominion over the fish of the sea, over the birds of the air, and over the cattle, over all the earth and over every creeping thing that creeps on the earth*

It is true that humans show signs of being made in the image of God through their moral, spiritual, and intellectual nature, which no other being on earth owns.

But with the New Testament being the fulfilment of the Old Testament prophecies, the Messiah, with His Divine image coming to the earth specifically to reach out to men with a message from His Father, clearly highlights that man was indeed made for covenant communion with God in righteousness and holiness.

The essential nature of mankind's spiritual relationship with the Godhead initiated by that breath of the Spirit into Adam's nostrils, is so clearly stated in the teaching given by the Messiah to Nicodemus and the woman-at-the-well (Jn. 4:21 – 24), endorsing the image of

God within man.

What is more the very fact that the Son came to earth in human flesh clearly confirms the fact that man was made in the image of God for He was able to easily inhabit a body of human flesh, which he would not have been able to do had we not been made in His image.

While the Fall marred that image – shattering the righteousness and holiness in which state we were first made – the objective of God in sending his Son, named Jesus Christ on His birth as a human being, was not just to redeem mankind but also restore that image of God within us *"in true righteousness and holiness" (Eph. 4:24)*.

Regarding the Christ who came in human form Paul wrote, *He is the image of the invisible God, the firstborn over all creation (Col. 1:15)* which also confirms the position of mankind as being in the image of God, for the Christ could not have appeared as a man without that clear, unambiguous connection.

Indeed the appearance of the Son of God in a human body on the earth, enabled Him to declare that He also became the Son of Man thus bringing into focus the whole purpose of God in creating man. That He loved man to the extent that the Father was prepared to allow His Son to be sacrificed in order for a pathway to be created that would allow man to return to Him and re-enter into communion with Him. But by establishing the means whereby man could reconnect with God

Paul establishes without doubt the position of the Messiah within the eternal Godhead as the Son of God when he wrote:

> *For by Him all things were created that are in heaven and on earth, both the visible and invisible, whether thrones or dominions or principalities or powers. All things were created through Him and for Him. (Col. 1:16)*

Not only was He responsible for the creation, but Paul clearly states that *He is before all things*, that is because nothing was present when the Son was with the Father and the Spirit in happy isolation. They were in no need of anyone else because they were completely self-sufficient

Not only was the Son responsible for speaking the Word of the Father, which the Sprit caused to become a reality, *all things were created*

19

that are in heaven and on earth, both the visible and invisible, whether thrones or dominions or principalities or powers, and once they were created and established they had all the power necessary for their maintenance.

Where Paul says that *in Him all things consist,* it means that all things have all the characteristics required by the one who created them out of nothing, and can just as easily be destroyed by Him.

And He is before all things, and in Him all things consist.

Then Paul brought in the Lord's future role in respect to all those who would not just believe in Him, but have a desire to follow Him within the body of believers through the statement *And He is the head of the body, the church.*

There is no doubt that the uniqueness of Christ must be continually emphasized to avoid the Lord being brought down from His exalted position as God by familiarity, as some, possibly in ignorance, are seeking to do. Because He instigated the church through the means of salvation He provided, so that all those who are saved by the shedding of His blood become members of the church He founded, he has become the head of that church.

Because Adam, the first man, sinned by rebelling against the direct command of God regarding the forbidden tree, it is very clear that only a man, albeit a perfect man — that is one who is completely sinless, completely compliant with the rules and laws laid down from the beginning by God — could die in man's stead to pay the price of that sentence of death imposed by the Father because of the sin of Adam.

Such is the Father's love for mankind in general and individual man in particular, that He gave His Son the task of becoming a man and dying as the Passover lamb. That emphasizes, as far as the Father is concerned, the fact that the man He created is like Him and to be rescued to enable them to become at one with Him as was His original intention. God and the image of Him reunited.

Did not the Lord pray that amazing prayer: *that they* (that is all those that truly believe in Him) *may be one, as You, Father, are in Me, and I in You; that they also may be one in Us.* Which would be impossible if we were not created in His image

And He is the head of the body, the church, who is the

20

beginning, the firstborn from the dead, that in all things He may have the preeminence.

Jesus is indeed *the head of the body, the church* because He is its founding principle, the whole reason for its existence. The Passover Lamb in His person joins transformed spiritual Gentiles to those Jews who have become the essence of spiritual Israel by accepting Him as their Messiah.

He is also *the beginning*, for He is eternal and because of His death in a human body and resurrected in that body, which was turned into a spiritual body whilst it was lying in the tomb, he became *the firstborn from the dead.*

The whole purpose of His mission to the earth was to establish the total power of God over all things, even life itself. So in dying and rising again He showed that God had compete control over His life so *that in all things He may have the preeminence* the superiority over all those who have been created.

> *For it pleased the Father that in Him all the fullness should dwell, and by Him to reconcile all things to Himself, whether things on earth or things in heaven, having made peace through the blood of His cross (Col. 1:19, 20).*

Such is the Father's love for the Son that He has established Him as the source and embodiment of His love and concern for man leading to their salvation. In fact *it pleased the Father that in Him* that is in Christ *all the fullness* of the Godhead *should dwell*, confirming that He is fully Divine even though for a time He was clothed in human flesh which was transformed into a spiritual body, upon His resurrection. At no time was His Divinity diminished, because He is eternally an intrinsic part of the Godhead.

The Father, is the authority within the Godhead, for the Son does all that the Father has instructed Him to say and do, and the Holy Spirit fulfils the word of the Son of God. Therefore, according to what Paul says to the Colossians, the Father has put His Son in position *to reconcile all things to Himself.*

Now the word reconcile is a very interesting word because it means to enable two apparently incompatible things to exist together, and those two things are sinful man and God. Sin separated man from God because the purity of God and the evil of the sinfulness of man caused a barrier to come between the two meaning they were irreconcilable.

But that reconciliation affects things on the earth and things in heaven [*whether things on earth or things in heaven*], it is an all-encompassing reconciliation for He has made peace *through the blood of His cross,* that is by dying as a perfect human being, as Adam was at first, He not only showed us what is possible but in dying as a perfect man, the blood He shed paid the price of man's rebellion against God that attracted the sentence of death in the first place.

3 THE BIRTH OF ISRAEL

The Rescue God

After the Earth descended into paganism, God decided to dispense with the man He had created. But out of the whole population on the earth at that time Noah was found to have a heart for God. And, to the amusement of many people, who ignored the warnings of impending disaster, Noah started to build an ark that would house many animals and his whole family for about a year.

The horror for the inhabitants of the world came with the rains and the drowning of the whole of mankind then living with the exception of Noah, his family members and all the animals housed in the ark that was saved from judgement by the waters of judgement.

It was when the ark came to rest and the family members were freed to farm the land that permission was given for man to eat meat. But in giving that permission God had a greater salvation in mind; that of the death of His Son. That was the first time the preciousness of blood was announced for in Genesis 9 God related it to life.

> *3 Every moving thing that lives shall be food for you. I have given you all things, even as the green herbs.*
> *4 But you shall not eat flesh with its life, that is, its blood.*
> *5 Surely for your lifeblood I will demand a reckoning; from the hand of every beast I will require it, and from the hand of man. From the hand of every man's brother I will require the life of man.*

In these verses God established the sacredness of blood right

23

from the start of this new chapter of the human race, with the promise that God would never again cause the earth to be flooded to the same extent.

In creating man as He did, and breathing into his nostrils spiritual life in order for man and God to communicate with each other, God desired that man should be blessed. It was the rebellion of man that caused the separation of God and man, but God was still determined to work with and through man.

When once again man went the way of worldly pleasures and the worship of pagan gods, not realizing that he was under the influence of Satan, God decided to select one man who would be the start of a nation through which He would speak to the world and illustrate through them the true way of life. This also created a history of man in relationship with God from which we, in the modern times, could understand how we must approach and relate to God.

It is sensible to assume that Abram was inwardly dissatisfied with the worship of pagan deities and the plethora of gods and goddesses then abounding. Although God could not look upon sin, the Holy Spirit was active in the world and able to see into the minds and hearts of individuals.

Exactly how God reached out to Abram we will never know but Abram responded and there must have been something about Abram that caused him to believe in this unknown and unseeable God for him to respond in the way he did.

Since Adam's disastrous rebellion, God has tested the willingness of man to be true to Him, as much for the benefit of the individual as to His own need of reassurance.

Abram was tested throughout his wanderings through what would eventually be the promised land for his offspring. Allowing Lot to choose the lush plains with the rougher terrain left to him was a test of the faith of Abram that he could rely on God supplying all his needs. His willingness to be a sojourner in the land that would never be his, but would be owned by his offspring according to the promise of God, was outstanding.

Not only did Abram have to wait until he was 100 years old for a son and heir, but was then tested as to his commitment to God by being instructed to sacrifice that precious and long awaited son on the mountain on which eventually the temple would be built. His willingness to be completely obedient to the will and purposes of

God sets him apart from most believers.

Again the lamb, the symbol God adopted for himself as a shepherd of the sheep, a male caught by its horns in the thicket was sacrificed in the place of his son Isaac, symbolic of the sacrifice of God's Son for all mankind as the Lamb of God (Jn. 1:29). God's plan of salvation had started to be set out in the lives of those chosen of God. This is God's handy work gradually being revealed through the lives of individuals.

With Abram being the first Hebrew, it was not until the third generation that a tribe began to take shape. But the rise of Jacob was not easy as he was the younger of the twins born to Rebekah.

However we see in what Rebekah was told by God concerning the elder serving the younger and what happened in regard to the clear concerns of Jacob regarding the oversight of the tribe through his challenge to Esau's birthright and being pushed into claiming the promise reserved for the elder son from his father, the pronouncement of God becoming reality.

The deception, arranged and promoted by Rebekah was clearly of God for Jacob did not try to disguise his voice although Rebekah had the foresight of putting the deceiving skins on Jacob's arms and neck. He was clearly God's choice, as is confirmed later when we learn that Jacob was loved of God whereas Esau, being a man of the world, was not loved by God (Ro. 9:30). Thus Rebekah did what was necessary to secure Jacob's future as the leader of the tribe through which God would reach out to the world.

In the case of Abraham's two sons the choice was clear. As Paul told the Galatians, one was the son of a slave woman, the other was the God enabled son, the son of His promise. One was the result of the interference of Sarai, the other was of God.

With regard to the preferment of Jacob, it was the choice between a man of the world in Esau or a man seen by God as one after His own heart in Jacob. It was the resilience of Jacob in acquiring the beautiful but pagan preferring Rachel after fourteen years which caused such rivalry between her and the less beautiful but devoted Leah.

It is clear that the reproductive abilities of Jacob's two main wives, Leah and Rachel, was according to their willingness to surrender themselves to the God of Jacob.

With Leah, knowing that she was not loved to the same degree as

Rachel because she was the result of her father's deception, yet her willingness to surrender herself to Jacob and the God he worshipped, God ensured that six of the sons were born to her, including Judah, the tribe of the Messiah, along with a daughter.

Rachel, on the hand could not let go of the family gods, stealing them when Jacob had to flee his father-in-law. Although she was allowed to bear two sons, one of whom was Joseph who was to rule Egypt, she died and was buried on route in a grave by an oak tree, not in the family burial place where Leah was buried.

It was the struggle Jacob had with the angel on his journey home to his father that finally secured for him a place in the heart of God when his name was changed from Jacob, meaning supplanter, to Israel, meaning fighter with God, after He struggled with the angel at the ford Jabbok.

The Birth of Israel

Four hundred years in Egypt, with many of those years being spent in slavery to one of the Pharaohs, is a divinely appointed time, with the four hundred year period occurring a number of times in the scriptures.

We have had Noah, Abram and Jacob, all outstanding men of God in their time. Now it is the turn of Moses who was born after the Pharaoh had decreed that all male children had to be killed.

Of Jacob's twelve sons only Joseph had a heart for God as had his father and it got him into a lot of trouble, ending up with him being sold into slavery. But all the while God was directing his path. His unwillingness to give up on the Lord his God, even as his world seemed to crumble, getting worse and worse, is a salutary lesson to us all, especially when he so skillfully handled the education of his brothers after the way they treated him when he disclosed to them the dreams he had received from God concerning them bowing to him.

It was Judah who showed his true self in his defense before Joseph, before Joseph revealed who he was.

Now we discover that a couple of the tribe of Levi, during the time of slavery, have a boy child born to them, which they secretly nurtured until the child was too big to hide. This son is a chosen child of God with a mighty task to perform for which he must be trained.

Moses is weaned by his mother and taught the things of God by his father before being adopted by a daughter of the Pharaoh. Something that only God could have achieved.

In the royal household he would have received privileged treatment and learned about royal life and received the best teaching in the land, ultimately entering the army and having command training.

At the age of forty he felt drawn by the Holy Spirit to his people and in the process of trying to look after them murdered an Egyptian and had to flee the country, ending up in the wilderness which would be his home for another forty years.

The purpose of this time looking after his father-in-law's sheep was for him to get familiar with that whole area along with the responsibility of leading a flock of sheep in preparation for leading the people of God through the wilderness.

When fully trained, he noticed a bush that appeared to be burning but was full of the glory and righteousness of God. In that holy place Moses was commissioned as the leader of His people Israel, only very reluctantly taking up the post.

Convincing the Hebrew leaders of his authenticity, with the assistance of his elder brother Aaron, Moses met with the Pharaoh to have him release God's chosen people from slavery.

During the battle between Moses and the Pharaoh, Moses gradually gained confidence becoming more and more angry at the Pharaoh's recalcitrant response to his increasing attempts to demonstrate the power of God over the gods and goddesses of Egypt. Finally it came to the tenth and final plague in which God would demonstrate His complete power over life itself.

It would also introduce a festival that was to be celebrated throughout all their generations until God provided another Saviour. Indeed the importance of the Passover cannot be overstated because in God's Plan the sacrifice of His Son was to happen on that very day many centuries later.

Every detail of that last meal in servitude was detailed and had to be performed exactly as prescribed. Keeping the lamb for three days, killing the lamb and the daubing its blood around the door of their homes, the roasting of the lamb symbolizing the burning of the sin offering, that no bone was to be broken, but that all the flesh had to be eaten up so that there was nothing left for the wild and abandoned pet animals to feed on. These were symbolic of the final sin offering when the Messiah was put to death before rising again.

This was God's plan to reflect what would happen when the Messiah was killed on the cross at calvary. Although the people of that time had no idea what would come to their people all those years later, yet it was important for them at that time because it meant that they were to be released from slavery.

The journey to the promised land could have been undertaken in eleven days, but first of all those who were not in tune with God and rebelled against Him and against Moses His chosen servant had to be culled. When the Hebrew slaves were released, in the chaos there would have been many others who took advantage of leaving Egypt. So it was a mixed bunch that left the land of Goshen.

God knew that the Pharaoh, once he had recovered from the shock of losing his eldest son, would have become angry and want to reverse his decision to release his workforce. With all the people and their animals moving very slowly and with the Red Sea to cross the chances of the Pharaoh catching up with them was very high.

Not only had God shown His mighty power through all the plagues, but He was about to perform another miracle that would permanently remove the legal obligation the Pharaoh had over His people. When Jacob came to Egypt he acknowledged the rule of the Pharaoh's, the kings of Egypt, over his people. By the Pharaoh not releasing His people his authority over them remained.

By holding the Egyptian army at bay whilst His people crossed the Red Sea on dry land, God ensured the safety of His people before allowing the Egyptians to cross after them but causing them to drown by allowing the sea to return to its former place by the time the army got halfway. With the Pharaoh and his heir dead, their authority over the children of Israel was removed.

During the next forty years through testing, the people of Israel were purified of all decenters and made ready to enter into the Promised land.

Although Moses had become close to God, and he was still very fit, He had become psychologically drained so God took him and caused him to be buried in an unmarked grave that could not be visited or worshipped at by later generations.

The Promised land

The initial success with the fall of Jericho was followed by the disaster of the battle for Ai. The people gained so much confidence in their success at Jericho that they took it into their own hands to approach the battle of Ai with just a few of the men without consulting God, and lost the battle.

Joshua tore his clothes and fell on his face before the ark of the Lord until evening. Then he did something that was entirely unbecoming of such a leader. He complained to the Lord.

> *"Why have you brought us over the Jordan to deliver us into the hands of the Amorites to destroy us? O Lord, what shall I say when Israel turns its back before its enemies? For the Canaanites and all the inhabitants of the land will hear it, and surround us, and cut off our name from the earth. Then what will You do for Your great name?" (Joshua 7:7 – 9)*

After all they had been through and how God had brought them to the promised land and given them victory over the city of Jericho, how come Joshua made such a complaint against God? After all it was they who had not consulted with God before planning to take the city of Ai, and yet it was His land that He was giving, yes giving to them.

All the treasure rescued from Jericho was to be given to the house of the Lord, for it was God who had given the city into their hands. But something happened of which the majority were totally unaware.

Achan had seen a beautiful Babylonian garment, two hundred shekels of silver and a wedge of gold weighing fifty shekels which he coveted and hid in his tent under the earth. The Lord saw it and withheld his help and protection when the reduced force went into battle for the city of Ai they were bound to fail because the Spirit of the Lord was not with them.

It was only by the Lord leading them to the culprit and him being convicted and punished along with his whole household that the Lord's anger was calmed. Then, instead of just a few men going into battle for the city of Ai, the whole army of the Israelites were employed with critical tactics that first lured all the fighting men out of the city and then a party of men went into the city and set it alight, at which time the army of Israel turned on the fighting men and slaughtered them. So the city of Ai was given into the hands of Israel.

Sadly throughout the conflict mistakes were made and not all the inhabitants were slaughtered as God required meaning that within them there was this thorn in the side that was to trouble Israel for the rest of its history.

Certainly the area of the Promised land shrank over time and even today there are parts of the original Promised land that are no longer under Israeli control.

The Judges

Such was the disastrous state of affairs within Israel that it was a case of every man for himself. Not a very good start in the promised land. There seemed to have been no one of the standing of Moses or Joshua to take over the ruling of the land and no sign of the high priest to take over the role of providing spiritual guidance and keeping the people focused on God.

In the stead of a leader or spiritual guide there came to prominence judges who ruled for a time before dying and the land reverting to a country without any cohesion, susceptible to incursions and raids by bandit groups. Each time of catastrophe the people would bear with it for a time and then cry out to God to save them. But each time He saved them they became complacent and forgot to worship Him as they should have done and He withdrew His protection from them so that it became a never ending cycle of events.

The final judge was Samuel whose story is quite remarkable.

Eli the high priest was very fat and getting old such that he had his two sons to take over the priestly duties. Sadly they were not God focused and corrupt, causing the people to no longer want to be involved with God in regard to the sacrifices and their dedication to the Lord lapsed.

Exactly the same is happening now for the clergy are pursuing alternative gospels and many are accommodating the social norms rather than teaching and preaching the true word of God.

The first wife of a man called Elkanah was named Hannah, but she was barren and having to take a lot of grief from his second wife called Penninah who had given birth to children. One day when close to the tabernacle in Shiloh. She was praying at the tabernacle with tears for a son who she promised to dedicate to the Lord.

It happened that soon after she fell pregnant and God caused her to give birth to a son whom she called Samuel, meaning God has heard, for she said I have asked for him from the Lord. What this means is that even with corruption and turmoil in the tabernacle and the country as a whole, there were still some souls truly dedicated to the Lord known as the remnant.

After weaning him, true to her word to the Lord, Hannah presented him to Eli to serve God in the tabernacle. The child grew and received a message from the Lord that spelt the end of the Eli dynasty. Samuel became central to the saving of Israel from the dominance of the Philistines, but his sons, like the sons of Eli, were evil in all their ways.

Of Jacobs 12 sons only Joseph knew the Lord their God. Eli was unable to train his sons to love the Lord and the same with Samuel even though he was truly a man of God. It is very clear that the sons do not necessarily follow the beliefs of the father, however spiritual their fathers are.

This failure of the sons of the high priests led to the people asking for a king to rule over them, which we will consider in another chapter.

4 GOD'S PLAN OF SALVATION

We need to consider Moses in more detail because he was instrumental in laying down the instructions and statutes given to him by God for the regulation of the life of the Israelites, starting with the ten commandments.

Chosen of God from birth and trained by God for his forthcoming role as leader of the Israelites, he had to quickly learn to trust God as the plagues got more severe. In fact it was after the third plague that he took charge, no longer requiring the assistance of Aaron to hold the rod or to speak for him.

In fact so successful was he in taking up the role that he got angry with Pharaoh's obstinate stance in reneging on his promise to release the people. However, it was with the last plague that he got the Israelites engaged and motivated with the purchasing and preparation of the lamb for the very first Passover.

The object of the Passover was to save all the firstborn from death, because God wanted to send a message to the Pharaoh that He held the lives of all men in His hands. It was also not only to cause the Pharaoh to release His people, but for the heir of the kingdom to die so that when the Pharaoh himself died, whilst chasing after the Israelites to recapture them, there was no heir to retain the authority of the Pharaoh over the people of Israel.

As Moses had got into his stride with serving God, when the Israelites left Goshen and started on their journey, it was Moses who, when the distant sand cloud caused by the army of the Pharaoh began getting nearer to them, reassured the people.

Holding out his arm over the sea for it to part giving them access to a dry sea floor on which to cross over the sea the pilar of cloud that was their guide during all their wanderings in the wilderness went behind them to prevent the Egyptian army from getting anywhere near His fleeing people.

Throughout the initial time pre-their marriage to God on Mount Sinai, it was Moses who went before the Lord their God to find out what he needed to do to sweeten the waters a Marah, to provide meat in the form of quails, and mana from heaven for food.

It was at Mount Sinai that Moses really came to his own by being the link between the people and God. It was a very special pre-marriage ceremony that was held. The binding of Israel to the God who first chose Abram, then Isaac and then Jacob. It represented the commissioning of Israel as His people through whom God would speak to the world.

> 3 And Moses went up to God, and the Lord called to him from the mountain, saying, "Thus you shall say to the house of Jacob, and tell the children of Israel:
>> 4 'You have seen what I did to the Egyptians, and how I bore you on eagles' wings and brought you to Myself.
>> 5 Now therefore, if you will indeed obey My voice and keep My covenant, then you shall be a special treasure to Me above all people; for all the earth is Mine.
>> 6 And you shall be to Me a kingdom of priests and a holy nation.'
> These are the words which you shall speak to the children of Israel."

And on hearing these words the people responded, "All that the Lord has spoken we will do."

Then the Lord required all the people to consecrate, and purify themselves for on the third day, [three being God's holy number], God would speak to them in person. This was a momentous moment when the creator God would speak to the people directly, giving them the ten commandments. When the Lord God descended onto the mountain there were peels of thunder along with lightening and a voice coming from out of a thick dark cloud covering the mountain. It was the voice of God speaking directly to the people.

He gave them the ten commandments which were to provide instructions on the way they were to conduct their daily lives, starting with the commitment to put God first in everything.

> 2 *"I am the Lord your God, who brought you out of the land of Egypt, out of the house of bondage.*
> 3 *"You shall have no other gods before Me.*

Their commitment to the one who had rescued them from bondage in Egypt was to be total for He had a special work for them to do in publishing His name throughout all the nations of the world. He wanted to bless them and make them into a great nation providing they acknowledged Him as their one true and only God.

He wanted to rid the world of the worship inspired by Satan and the angels that fell from heaven with him, which were represented by carved images of the creatures and things that God had created rather than the creator.

> 4 *"You shall not make for yourself a carved image with any likeness to anything that is in heaven above, or in the earth beneath, or that is in the water under the earth;*
> 5 *you shall not bow down to them nor serve them.*

The Lord God had every right in His own world that He had created from nothing to be worshipped, not for His own ego but in recognition that He was the Father of us all. All the while men focused their attention on Him there would be a bonding built up between individuals and God resulting in love bringing the two together.

For God knew that the life of man was eternal and only those who worshipped Him as their God would have access to His eternal rest, with all those that refused to worship Him confined to a place devoid of His presence and therefore filled with hate and anger and corruption and without His light.

> *For I, the Lord your God, am a jealous God, visiting the iniquity of the fathers upon the children to the third and fourth generations of*

those who hate Me,

This did not mean that God would actually visit the guilt upon the children to the third and fourth generation, but that as the children were brought up hating the things of God, that is what would happen. There was always the chance of a child bucking the system to give glory to God.

> *6 but showing mercy to thousands, to those who love Me and keep My commandments.*

This is the Love of God is action, to love those that love Him in return. That is why He made man in the first pace and why He made him in His image, so that there would be easy intercourse between them and He would provide for them and lavish His love upon them.

> *7 "You shall not take the name of the Lord your God in vain, for the Lord will not hold him guiltless who takes His name in vain.*

Because of His position as our creator and benefactor it is essential that we treat the name of the Lord our God with absolute respect.

God's promise of protection was an essential element of their coming together, for, although they were unaware of it at the time God's intended eternal sacrifice for salvation was to be through this nation. As the Lord Jesus told the Samaritan woman, *'salvation is of the Jews'*.

So after giving them instructions for the three major festivals God told the people through Moses that His angel would go before them to be an enemy to their enemies and an adversary to their adversaries.

In return they had to obliterate all the pagan tribes they encountered, destroying all their sacred pillars. This was to prepare the land for the children of Israel to live in a close relationship with their holy God.

It was at this time that God instructed Moses to produce a tabernacle that would symbolize His presence amongst them, although as Solomon was to announce when commissioning the permanent temple he built to the glory of God (2 Chron. 6:18),

> *"But will God indeed dwell with men on the earth? Behold, heaven and the heaven of heavens cannot contain You. How much less this temple which I have built!*

However this tabernacle that Moses was told to produce was the exact copy of the tabernacle in heaven and through its design provided the people with the way of salvation, although they did not recognize it as such[3] at the time. The entrance to the courtyard was the starting point, which demonstrated a willingness to interact with God.

Then came the altar of sacrifice where a sacrifice for their confessed sins was burned. The laver initially filled with clear water became dirty with the hand washing of the priests, signaling that sin contaminating the water.

Next came the two compartment tabernacle, or Tent of the Meeting. In the first part was the candelabra with a central stem and two sets of three stems either side of the central stem making seven stems in all, with seven denoting spiritual perfection and the hall mark of the Holy Spirit. The central stem represents God who is the light of life with the six[4] side branches representing man in his righteous state (for more detail see my book The Tent of the Meeting).

The altar of incense represents the prayers of the saints because prayer is essential in our relationship with God, it is the way we commune with God.

The table of shewbread carried twelve newly baked shewbread made of fine flour and representing each of the tribes of Israel which were made holy by being in His presence. They were made with unleavened flour (uncontaminated with sin).

In the second, inner compartment was the ark of the covenant over which was the mercy seat, and only the high priest could enter with the blood of sacrifice on his hands once a year on the day of atonement to plead for the people.

The priest themselves, who were priests to God and therefore the intermediaries between God and men and the only ones allowed to serve at the altar of burnt offering and in the tabernacle, had to wear special garments that covered their whole body so that no flesh was

---

[3] Please read my book The Tent of the Meeting ; Illustrating God's Plan of Salvation.
[4] Six is man's number because he was created on day six.

exposed. They were holy garments to be worn only during the various services.

The high priest wore a turban with a gold plate over it inscribed with the words 'Holiness to the Lord', which was located over his forehead. The forehead was a sacred place to God for it is on the forehead that all true believers will receive a mark *"Then I looked, and behold, a Lamb standing on Mount Zion, and with Him one hundred and forty-four thousand, having His Father's name written on their foreheads."* (Rev. 14:1)

Various sacrificial services were laid out and to be followed religiously, all honouring God, with the sin offering being the most important.

This was the start of the process of allowing the people to get right with God. And when camped the tabernacle would be in the centre of the camp, causing the people to recognize the centrality of God in their lives.

Sadly, in spite of all that God had done for them, even to hearing His voice so spectacularly speaking to them from the mountain, there were still some who were unbelieving and rebellious.

At one time Moses was summoned to the mountain by God and was with the Lord for forty days and nights listening to God and collecting the two tablets of stone provided by God with the ten Hebrew words, representing the ten commandments, inscribed on them by God's own hand.

It was that absence of Moses for such a long time that caused the rebels to persuade Aaron to create the image of a golden calf for them to worship, thus taking them back in time to when they were in Egypt worshipping idols and pagan symbols, completely forgetting all the freedom and promises God had given to them. There are some people who will never believe in God whatever proof He was able to give to them.

This was to be the trigger for a major pruning of the people who came out of Egypt, for God mentioned to Moses that all was not well back in camp. He was so angry with them that He threatened to wipe them out and use Moses as the first of a new Israel until Moses pacified Him saying that it would not work well because the other nations would consider the escape from Egypt a failure.

When Moses came down from his time with God on the mountain and saw what was going on he threw down the tablets of stone breaking them, but the covenant was already broken by the action of the people.

He then burned the idol with fire and ground down the image to a powder, put it in the water and made them drink it. Then turning to Aaron he demanded to know what made him create such an abominable image and cause the people to sin. Aaron's excuse was entirely flimsy but Moses managed to gain forgiveness from God for him, but his leadership was compromised from there on.

Moses then called for all those who had not sinned and were on the side of the Lord to come to him and all the Levites came to him. He then ordered them to done swords and kill all those who worshipped the golden calf image even their own brethren; which numbered 3,000.

This may seem severe but this was the training period for the Children of Israel when only those who were prepared to love and serve the Lord their God would survive. All those who rebelled against God or His servant Moses were beyond salvation and bound for hell, their lives pointless.

By the Levites being prepared to kill all those opposed to God and all that He had planned for the people in the future, it gained them a blessing because they did not spare even their brethren in the service of the Lord.

The Lord is a God of love for all those prepared to worship and serve Him, but to those that oppose Him only eternal death awaits them. After all it is His world and we were made by Him, therefore if we do not praise and glorify our creator and Lord then we are not worthy of Him taking care of us. It is our choice.

Having smashed the first lot of tablets of stone, Moses was required to dig out two more tablets, which with the basic tools they had to use would have taken a considerable time. It was then Moses task to take them up the mountain for God to inscribe the ten Hebrew words on them.

This new set were to be safely stored in an ark of wood covered with gold as the people's record of their covenant with God.

Moving on from Mount Sinai The Israelites were to face many more testing times before reaching the promised land, with the biggest test being their ability to trust God. That time came when they were faced with the possibility of them going into the promised land.

Sending in twelve spies, one from each tribe, this party scouted the length and breadth of the land giving a report on their return. Yes the land was all that the Lord said it was, a land flowing with milk and honey and even bringing back huge bunches of grapes to prove what they saw, but the report they gave of the people and their walled cities was enough to put the people off going in.

Even with God saying that He would be going in with them, and with all the mighty power and provisioning He had proven He could supply, after getting them out of Egypt, crossing the Red Sea and the many other examples of His ability to overcome their difficulties they still did not fully trust Him. Hearing the report of ten of the spies that the opposition from mighty men of valour and behind their walled cities there was far too much for them to overcome so the people refused to go in.

Just two spies, Joshua and Caleb, were the only ones urging the people that God was able to overcome the opposition and were prepared to trust God and go in to conquer the land. But because of their lack of trust in Him, God consigned the people to a total of forty years in the wilderness so that all those who were still of a slave mentality and unable to trust God to assist them overcome the people would have died out with the exception of those that had been prepared to trust God.

The people were to face many more tests, before reaching the border to the promise land.

5 MOSES

Perhaps one of the greatest prophets that has ever lived who had no idea of all that God had planned for him to do when he met with the Lord at the burning bush.

God had trained him well, although Moses had no idea of his potential when he reluctantly accepted the task of leading the Israelites out of bondage and to the border of the promised land. Although he led them well, the stresses and strains made upon him, mentally and psychologically with their constant complaining, built up so that towards the end he made some mistakes which suggested to the Lord that he was no longer fit to be leader. He had done a remarkable job in leading them but it was clear that it was time for a younger person to take over.

But his legacy is eternal for he laid the foundations of the way of life not only for those that were to govern the lives of the children of Israel throughout their generations, but are as important today in the way we approach and serve God.

Moses the Mediator

Moses became like the mother hen, protecting the people he led although willing to take firm and decisive action against rebels.

From the start Moses gained strength of character dealing with the Pharaoh to the extent that he was definitely in control by the time of the Passover. As soon as Pharaoh gave permission for the release of the slaves and the mobilization started, Moses was at the front leading the people out of bondage.

When it came to facing the Red Sea Moses calmed the fears of the people and pointing his staff over the sea the people saw it parting and the pilar of cloud pass from in front of them to behind them blinding the Egyptians and stopping them overtaking the people of the Lord. When they had passed through the sea, they saw the sea return to normal drowning the Egyptian army and the Pharaoh.

Moses led the Israelites in praise of their God who had saved them so dramatically.

His mediatorial skills started soon afterwards, for in spite of what they had witnessed, the people seemed to have short memories. As soon as they encountered a difficult situation like no drinkable water they immediately relapse into complaining mode. With the new relationship Moses had gained with the Lord he quickly passed the problem to Him, and was guided to put a tree into the water to purify it.

But then the people complained too much and God was furious with them and sent fire amongst the camp and they cried out to Moses who prayed to the Lord and the fire was stopped.

They then complained about their diet of Manna, saying that they remembered the fish and vegetables and fruit they ate in Egypt without mentioning the hard labour they had to endure that had caused them to cry out to the Lord to save them.

But their crying out laid heavily upon Moses and he in turn complained to the Lord that the burden was too heavy on him.

10 Then Moses heard the people weeping throughout their families, everyone at the door of his tent; and the anger of the Lord was greatly aroused; Moses also was displeased.

11 So Moses said to the Lord, "Why have You afflicted Your servant? And why have I not found favor in Your sight, that You have laid the burden of all these people on me?

12 Did I conceive all these people? Did I beget them, that You should say to me, 'Carry them in your bosom, as a guardian carries a nursing child,' to the land which You swore to their fathers?

13 Where am I to get meat to give to all these people? For they weep all over me, saying, 'Give us meat, that we may eat.'

14 I am not able to bear all these people alone, because the burden is too heavy for me.

15 If You treat me like this, please kill me here and now, if I have found favor in Your sight, and do not let me see my wretchedness!"

Through this pleading with the Lord, the Lord commissioned seventy men to share the burden with him, and then the Lord caused a wind to blow quail and the people gathered in the quail. But the Lord also caused His anger to burn against them and many people died that day because their stomachs could not handle the gorging on the rich quail meat.

There were many other rebellions and complaints from the people and all resulted in swift action by God to deal with those who complained. But it was the constant complaining that got to Moses such that he made two errors of judgement leading to the Lord taking him before he could enter the promised land.

Moses the Teacher

5 Surely I have taught you statutes and judgments, just as the Lord my God commanded me, that you should act according to them in the land which you go to possess.

Throughout his leadership, particularly after their yearlong sojourn at Mount Sinai when they received the ten commandments from the mouth of God Himself, God started to give Him instructions about the way of life that the chosen people were expected to live and which he taught to the people. These regulations and statutes were to be followed to keep them close to God Himself and provide them with a life of blessing and protection.

Sadly it was whilst collecting the first tablets of stone God had personally provided, inscribed with the ten commandments that the people had Aaron make the Golden calf and the culling of the unbelieving rebellious people began.

At the end of his time as leader Moses gave three discourses[5] summing up all his teaching to the people regarding how they must conduct themselves in the promised land.

6 Therefore be careful to observe them; for this is your wisdom and your understanding in the sight of the peoples who will hear all these statutes, and say, 'Surely this great nation is a wise and

---

[5] A study of those discourses can be found in my book Deuteronomy

understanding people.' (Deut. 4)

The people were given the opportunity to be premier amongst the nations that would surround them in the promised land by being obedient to the statutes and judgements of God causing those nations to respect them and say, *'Surely this great nation is a wise and understanding people.*

He reminded them of what happened at Baal Peor when many of the young men and girls were drawn into worshipping the gods of the people and were killed as a result because God wanted them to demonstrate what He was able to do through a compliant and respectful people who believed in Him as their sole creator God.

> *7 'For what great nation is there that has God so near to it, as the Lord our God is to us, because for whatever reason we may call upon Him?*
> *8 And what great nation is there that has such statutes and righteous judgments as are contained in this law which I set before you this day?*
> *9 Only take heed to yourself, and diligently keep yourself, lest you forget the things your eyes have seen, and lest they depart from your heart all the days of your life. And teach them to your children and your grandchildren,*
>
> *(Deut. 4)*

Surely they were a favoured nation to have the Lord God, the creator of all things, as their God, guiding and protecting them amongst many hostile nations.

In the second discourse Moses went through the ten commandments explaining what was required of them starting with the iconic first of the ten which was, as the Son of God put it, for them to love the Lord their God:

> *29 Jesus answered him, 'The first of all the commandments is: 'Hear, O Israel, the Lord our God, the Lord is one.*
> *30 And you shall love the Lord your God with all your heart, with all your soul, with all your mind, and with all your strength.' This is the first and great commandment.*

Their commitment to God was to be uppermost in their minds and hearts, living their lives in respectful thanks to Him for rescuing them from slavery in Egypt and having no other gods but Him. The nations around them worshipped useless images, but because God was a Spirit being, no image could be made of Him and He deserved their total respect for He, as creator, was great and greatly to be praised.

The sabbath day, the seventh day when He rested, was His day and was decreed to be a day of rest when no work was done, giving the people time to meditate on Him and His word. God also knew that they would need at least one day of relaxation and recuperation per week.

The other commandments related to life in a nation, which at first would have been a foreign experience because in Egypt they were not a nation and since leaving Egypt they were semi-nomadic and not living as a static and secure nation.

But his main concern was not only the foundations of the covenant God made with them, but the spirit in which the covenant was to be kept and the right motives of those who sought to obey it.

Sadly the nation was unable to bring themselves to realize just how much of a distinction it was for them to have been chosen of God, instead desiring to be like all the other nations around them.

It was necessary for them to fear the Lord their God, not in terms of being frightened, more for them to show Him complete and unfettered respect, if for no other reason than that He created them, chose them, supported them and total respect for the awesome power He wielded.

The Peril of Forgetting

This need for every person to know the commandments, the rules that were to govern their life in the promised land, was for the relationship they had with God to be enhanced and become part of their natural way of life and thinking. Their 'religion' was not to be an add on, nor one where everything was done by rote, but to be the essence of their life before a loving and merciful God.

What is more it was important that they never forgot certain facts:

1. that it was God who had brought them to the land that He had sworn to give to the descendants of *Abraham, Isaac, and Jacob* because of the faithfulness of those men.

2. It was a land with great and splendid cities which they did not build.

3. The houses were full of all good things which they had not provided.

4. There were excavated cisterns (underground water reservoirs) which they had not dig out.

5. vineyards and olive trees which they did not plant.

6. they would eat and be full and satisfied. No further need of manna.

Having received the gift of so much of what they had not worked hard to build up, there was a very strong chance that they would not appreciate it and completely forget that it was *the Lord who brought you out of the land of Egypt, out of the house of slavery* and had provided all that there was for them to enjoy.

This brings to mind the thought that as sinners saved by the blood of the Lamb of God, we could well not appreciated all that God through Christ has done for us!

This is especially true of those who, having been told about salvation, have been led to understand all about it from scripture and accepted Christ as their Lord and Saviour, but then have not pursued the study of scripture, as the Israelites were being instructed to do, in order to gain a deeper and more solid understanding of all that the Lord had to go through in order to provide them with that salvation.

As the writer to the Hebrews (5:12 – 14) wrote:

> *For though by this time you ought to be teachers because of the time you have had to learn these truths, you still require someone to teach you again the elementary principles of God's word from the beginning, needing to be continually fed with milk like spiritual infants still at the breast, not solid food like spiritual adults who have studied the scriptures to fully understand what salvation is all about.*
>
> *Every believer who lives on milk is inexperienced on matters of doctrine and unskilled in the word of righteousness, since he is a*

spiritual infant. Solid food is for the spiritually mature, whose senses are trained by practice through the knowledge of the word of God to distinguish between what is morally good and what is evil.

How many of those who go to church, who regularly worship with other believers, really understand what being a member of spiritual Israel really means, if they even know what spiritual Israel is.

A relative, who had been brought up in the church with parents that both had lay positions in the church, had gone to Sunday School and was confirmed as a church member, bought a copy of my book The Tent of the Meeting and had to admit to me that she did not understand a word of it, yet it contained solid scripture from Genesis through to Revelation. After over seventy odd years in the church she did not know scripture except for superficial stuff. She was still just a babe needing to be bottle fed with babies milk.

Do such people really know what the Christian faith is all about or what they have to do to remain in that fold and not wander off like an errant sheep? After all there is always the chance that, like so many Israelites, they may be met with God rejecting them on the day of judgement with the words, *begone from me, I never knew you!*

Moving on we read about what they had to do to remain close to God.

13 You shall fear the Lord your God alone; and you shall serve Him with awe-filled reverence, profound respect and swear oaths by His name and His name alone. (Deut. 6)

You shall be fearful of not fully appreciating the power and ability of God to love and protect you. Although the charge of rebelliousness against God is always there over our heads because of Adam and the resulting DNA of sin that seeks to destroy us, God is constantly providing the antidote all the while we seek after Him *with awe-filled reverence,* and *with profound respect* worship Him only.

It is our focusing upon God who alone is able to block out the debilitating distractions of the world, thus enabling us to become united spiritually with God.

Separateness

One thing is certain and that is it is impossible to apply the current sense of skewed morality, which in far too many cases is a superficial thing, to the time of tribal conflict and the depths of crude, sexual and barbarous paganism to which the pagan nations had sunk.

In fact God had waited patiently until the land had become so defiled that he decided it was time for His chosen people to go in and purge the land of all its depraved moral corruption and as a centre of Satanic power.

Leave one person to whom this was normal, even a child, and there was every chance that that person would infect the weaker members of the house of Israel and then it would spread throughout the nation like a rampant disease. ~As the saying goes: one bad apple can infect a basket full of them, making the contents of the basket only fit to be thrown away.

Only those who have experienced the enormity of the love and presence of God know the difference between living according to God's laws and those of Satan.

> *3 You shall not intermarry with them. You shall not give your daughter to his son, nor take his daughter for your son; because being part of their family they will turn your sons away from following Me to serve other gods; then the anger of the Lord will be aroused and burn against you and He will quickly destroy you.*

A good illustration of this is Solomon who, against the commandments of God, married pagan wives with hundreds of pagan concubines and it was those wives and concubines who corrupted that once great man of God. Solomon's successor, Rehoboam was most likely the son of a pagan mother.

Spiritual warfare is no less cruel than physical warfare and is often hidden, like terrorism, being full of subterfuge.

It is also important to compare life in those parts of the world today under the dominance of barbarism, with bizarre killings, severe oppression through a police state and unelected leaders in the Middle East, especially with those living in peace and reasonable harmony within other more stable countries in the west.

The seven nations identified as being greater and mightier than the Israelites that God was going to help them conquer, had to be utterly destroyed. What we have to remember, not only in respect to the Israelites but also in respect to us as believers in the Lord Jesus

Christ, is that God is the final judge and it is incumbent upon us to be pure before Him, because it is possible that even people we know as friends, could well be amongst those whom the Lord rejects when He sits in judgement on the great white throne at the end of time.

> *5 But this is how you shall deal with them: you shall utterly destroy their altars and completely demolish their sacred pillars, and cut down their wooden images (such as the Asherim which were symbols of the goddess Asherah), and burn their carved or sculpted images in the fire.*

Like a cancer, one minute it will suddenly explode into life through the efforts of Satan and his demonic spirits to cause mayhem.

All those nations the Israelites were commanded to slaughter were people already bound for that place referred to as hell, and could do untold spiritual damage, not only to the people of God but could even seek to destroy His plan of salvation, therefore the people of Israel were ridding the world of those who served Satan and his fallen angels and dragging others down to their level.

In the Second Testament Martha was more interested in the practical matters of the home, whereas Mary wanted to sit at the feet of Jesus to learn spiritual truth (Lk. 10:38 – 42).

Isaiah was told to

> *"Go, and tell this people:*
> *'Keep on listening, but do not understand;*
> *Keep on looking, but do not comprehend.'*

The people just could not, would not understand that God was not in the physical. Yes the world was influence by Him. But God was far more than the physical. They had to search for Him using their minds and hearts. They had to want Him for Him to become real to them. Jacob had that searching heart and in a struggle with an angel discovered God.

Surely with all that had happened to the people of Israel and their forebears, their history should have taught them that God was not something physical, something visual that they could worship, but far deeper than that that it needed their understanding.

The words of the prophets were heard but not understood, because the people did not search for an understanding of what God was telling them through the prophets.

Choice of Life or Death

Deuteronomy is all about warnings, not only about the people's focus on the God that brought them out of slavery in Egypt, but also about the many dangers that they were to face when they went into inhabit the land and the dangers of departing from the word and way of God so clearly presented by Moses.

It is essential that we, today, remember this is all about the *choice* made available to us to repent of our sins and be washed in the blood of the Lamb. This whole subject matter is literally a fact of life or death, from a spiritual perspective, and therefore not to be taken lightly. It means having the opportunity to rejoice in heaven with God, or to be consigned to hell without any means of escape (Lk. 16:26).

It is not good to rely on others for spiritual teaching without knowing where they stand with God or looking it up for yourself, for we are all individually responsible for our own salvation. It is no good on the day of judgement saying, "Well that is what I was taught by the minister or lay preacher on Sundays." The choice between life and death is our responsibility alone. Only those who read the Word and through asking and reading what others have written and meditating what we read and seeking the face of God will we be able to discern the truth.

Consider the letters to the seven churches in Revelation[6]. The members of Ephesus had lost their love for the Lord that first persuaded them to believe, the members at Pergamon had allowed Nicolaitans who believed in sexual immorality and sacrificing to idols to work within the church. Then there was the church at Thyatira that allowed a self-confessed prophetess named Jezebel to teach and seduce members. The people at Sardis were spiritually dead, the people at Philadelphia were doing well facing the Jews in the synagogue of Satan and finally the Laodiceans were only lukewarm about their faith, neither hot nor cold and were about to be rejected by God.

---

[6] See my book, Letters to the Seven Churches of Revelation

It is important to notice that in Acts 20:27, Paul declares that *'I did not shrink from declaring to you <u>the whole purpose and plan of God.</u>'* Paul taught them the whole undiluted purpose and plan of God, but he did not do that in five or ten minute weekly sermons but through long sessions to those hungry for spiritual truth. A hunger for spiritual truth that is clearly absent in many churches today.

Indeed it has been my experience amongst so called Christians, that if I start to discuss the deep truths of the Christian gospel, far too many Christians either do not want to know what I was talking about, or were embarrassed, or had no idea what I am talking about.

It is essential that we, today, remember this is all about the *choice* made available to us to repent of our sins and be washed in the blood of the Lamb. This whole subject matter is literally a fact of life or death, from a spiritual perspective, and therefore not to be taken lightly. It means having the opportunity to rejoice in heaven with God, or to be consigned to hell without any means of escape (Lk. 16:26).

As Moses said to the people:

> *15 "Listen to me closely, I have set before you today life and prosperity, death and adversity, 16 in that I command you today to love the Lord your God, to walk in His ways, and to keep His commandments, His statutes, and His judgments, that you may live and multiply; and the Lord your God will bless you in the land which you go to possess.*
>
> *17 But if your heart turns away so that you do not hear, and you are drawn away to worship other gods and serve them, 18 I announce to you today that you shall surely perish; you shall not prolong your days in the land which you cross over the Jordan to go in and possess.*
>
> *19 I call heaven and earth as witnesses today against you, that I have set before you life and death, blessing and cursing; therefore you should choose life, that both you and your descendants may live (enjoy eternal life).*
>
> *20 That by loving the Lord your God as He has called you to do, you may obey His voice, and cling to Him, for He is your life and the length of your days;*

The Lord God of Israel, the creator of all that is, the creator and sustainer of all life, is calling upon all flesh to love Him and serve Him so that He might bless them and all that they do. For as our designer and creator He knows us better than we know ourselves.

We were created according to His design, we were given a spirit with which we can communicate with Him. It is an eternal spirit with two possible outcomes. Either to be with Him for eternity or to be in that place He has prepared for those who ignore or reject Him, also for eternity.

As Moses laid out in his book Deuteronomy, we have a choice of living the life God envisioned for us or to live a life in opposition to Him and die an eternal death.

6 THE KINGS OF ISRAEL AND JUDAH[7]

The corruption of the sons of Samuel resulted in the lack of true faith amongst most of the people in their God to look after them, therefore people turned aside from God, wanting to be like all the nations around them and have a king in spite of all the warnings concerning the requirements of a king.

1   Now when Samuel was old he made his sons judges over Israel...
3   But his sons did not walk in his ways; they turned aside after dishonest gain, took bribes, and perverted justice.
4   Then all the elders of Israel gathered together and came to Samuel and said to him, "Look, you are old, and your sons do not walk in your ways. Make us a king to judge us like all the nations."
(1 Sam. 8)

This is exactly what the Lord predicted through Moses in Deuteronomy 17:14 – 20.

6   Samuel was displeased when they said, "Give us a king to judge us." So Samuel prayed to the Lord who said to Samuel, "Heed the voice of the people in all that they say to you; for they have not rejected you, but they have rejected Me, that I should not reign over

---

[7] For a full understanding of the kings of Israel and Judah please see my book Law & Grace.

them.
8   According to all the works which they have done since I brought
them up out of Egypt, even to this day they have forsaken Me and
served other gods, so they are doing to you also.
9   Now therefore, heed their voice. However, you shall solemnly
forewarn them, and show them the behavior of the king who will
reign over them."

If the sons of Samuel did *not walk in your ways* what chance the sons of kings who will not have the same access to God as they did as priest of the most high God? They are still human and with kings ignoring God's instructions not to marry pagan wives it was inevitable that error would creep in and the kings be led astray from all that they had been taught through Moses.

But God with His foresight knew what would happen and had already planned the succession of His sacrificial Son to become king of Israel in succession to the only true servant of God, David.

Israel at that time had no standing army, just a territorial army called to arms when the country was in trouble, but with no leader this was a very ad hoc affair.

God chose for them a young man, both tall and handsome, to be their king whom they accepted and he was crowned the first king of Israel. But Saul was a very weak king with a very weak faith in God.

However God had another man who He had chosen to be king when he was of an age. David was a shepherd of his father's sheep with a very deep and profound faith in God. When he was still a young lad his father told him to take some food to his older brothers fighting the Philistines. He arrived at the time of Goliath issuing his great challenge. But there was no one brave enough to take him on.

David, full of trust in the power of the Lord of Hosts, decided to meet this Goliath in a contest with nothing more than a sling and five pebbles taken from a stream.

45   Then David said to the Philistine, "You come to me with a
sword, with a spear, and with a javelin. But I come to you in the
name of the Lord of hosts, the God of the armies of Israel, whom
you have defied.
46   This day the Lord will deliver you into my hand, and I will
strike you and take your head from you. And this day I will give

the carcasses of the camp of the Philistines to the birds of the air and the wild beasts of the earth, that all the earth may know that there is a God in Israel.

47 Then all this assembly shall know that the Lord does not save with sword and spear; for the battle is the Lord's, and He will give you into our hands."

(1 Sam. 17)

This was a youth who had battled with a lion and a bear and won, indeed he was fearless before this great giant of a man, running towards him he selected a stone form his pouch and slung the stone which penetrated the giants forehead and he fell down dead.

This led to David working for Saul, and becoming a mighty man of war. Returning from a battle the women came out with tambourines, dancing and singing that Saul had slain his thousands and David his ten thousands, which displeased the king, and he set out to kill David, but God rescued him and kept him safe. Finally Saul was killed in battle and David became king, initially just of Judah but then of the whole of Israel.

David was a man of great faith and knew God personally and succeeded in many battles causing many nations to become subservient to him and it was for Israel the greatest time in its history. But sadly his sons did not follow in his footsteps and because of his sin against Uriah the Hittite in taking his wife Bathsheba and causing him to be killed, David was punished during his final tenure as king being fraught with problems within his family.

David was able to save up a considerable fortune to build a temple to God which he was not allowed to build, but his successor Solomon was.

The Bible is excellent for teaching us how to live our lives with a multitude of lessons about what people in power did and didn't do and the result of those decisions they made.

Before Solomon came to the throne his father King David held a meeting with all the leaders of Israel to explain that although God had prevented him from building a Temple for the Lord, he had amassed a huge amount of material to be used to build the first permanent Temple to replace the transportable tabernacle made by Moses which had survived up to that time. God had also given David the plans for the construction of the Temple, as in the case of Moses' tabernacle, but which disappeared to prevent a replica being constructed later.

Consider the advice David gave his son, Solomon:

"And now, Solomon my son, learn to know the God of your father, and serve him with a singleness of mind and a willing heart; for the Lord thoroughly searches every mind, and understands every plan and thought.

If you seek him, he will be found by you (cf. Matt. 7:7);

but if you forsake him, he will abandon you forever.

Take this whole matter very seriously, because the Lord has chosen you to build a house as his sanctuary; therefore, be strong, and carry out the work." (1 Chron. 28:9, 10)

Also when David was near to death:

"he charged his son Solomon, saying: 'I am about to go the way of all flesh. Be strong, be courageous (cf. Joshua 1:9), and keep the charge of the Lord your God, walking in his ways and keeping his statutes, his commandments, his ordinances, and his testimonies, as it is written in the law of Moses, so that you may prosper in all that you do and wherever you turn. Then the Lord will establish his word that he spoke concerning me: 'If your heirs take heed to their way, to walk before me in faithfulness with all their heart and with all their soul, you will not fail to have a successor on the throne of Israel." (1 Kgs. 2:1 – 4)

With all this advice it was up to Solomon to become close to the Lord God of Israel and seek to be a faithful servant by obeying some basic rules provided by Moses in the book of Deuteronomy. Rules are meant to be read and applied if they are to be effective, the purity of the faith of any believer depends on it if they are to get close to God.

Not only did Solomon have his father as an example but also the history of Israel since their exodus from Egypt. All the time the people obeyed God they enabled Him to support and bless them, but as soon as they started to forget their God, particularly if they started to worship the gods of the surrounding nations, God withdrew His support and allowed other nations to subdue them.

Solomon started well through a wise judgement in a case brought to him by two prostitutes over a baby. But from then on in he became introspective and ignored the word of God.

> *17 Neither shall he multiply wives for himself, lest his heart turn away; nor shall he greatly multiply silver and gold for himself.*

Both these things he did by becoming exceptionally wealthy, and acquiring many pagan wives and concubines, totally ignoring these words of instruction from Deuteronomy.

> *18 "Also it shall be, when he sits on the throne of his kingdom, that he shall write for himself a copy of this law in a book, from the one before the priests, the Levites.*
> *19 And it shall be with him, and he shall read it all the days of his life, that he may learn to fear the Lord his God and be careful to observe all the words of this law and these statutes,*
> *20 so that his heart may not be lifted above his brethren, that he may not turn aside from the commandment to the right hand or to the left, and that he may prolong his days in his kingdom, he and his children in the midst of Israel.*
> *(Deut. 17)*

Young and new to the job Solomon realized that he was in dire need of help. We are told that Solomon loved the Lord, even to walking in the statutes of his father David with the exception that he sacrificed and burned incense at the alternative high places to the tabernacle.

When the Lord appeared to Solomon in a dream to ask him what he wanted, he very sensibly asked for an understanding heart to govern the people and know right from wrong (1 Kngs. 3:5 – 14). The Lord was pleased that he asked for wisdom and promised that he would be the most wise man ever along with riches and fame. The gift was proven when he successfully and inspirationally judged the two prostitutes and the living son.

If God had been able to establish and sustain the rule of his father David so effectively, why did Solomon need to make alliances with other nations which worshipped other gods? Was God not more powerful than many such nations?

Solomon's first major error was to enter into an alliance with Pharaoh by marrying one of his daughters. Why was this wrong? Not only was the king aligning himself with a pagan nation, for the Pharaoh considered himself a god and the Egyptians, as we know from the plagues, worshipped many gods, but by marrying one of his daughters she would want to continue to worship the gods she knew, therefore there was the potential for Solomon to be distracted from the worship of the God of Israel. Also the warning from God through Moses is relevant:

• *he must not acquire many wives for himself, or else his heart will be turned away.*

And what did Solomon do but marry many wives, mostly from the very tribes Israel should have annihilated when they went into the Promised Land because those tribes worshipped many gods but not the one true God (1 Kgs. 11:1 – 4). The cause of his fall from grace is undoubtedly not just the number of his wives but their ancestry:

The Lord was very angry with Solomon, because his heart had turned away from the Lord, the God of Israel, who had appeared to him twice. He had warned him concerning this matter, that he should not follow other gods; but he ignored what the Lord commanded.
Therefore the Lord said to Solomon, 'Since you have decided not to keep my covenant and have disobeyed my decrees, I will surely tear the kingdom from you and give it to one of your servants. Yet for the sake of your father David I will not do it in your lifetime; I will tear it out of the hand of your son. I will not, tear away the entire kingdom; I will give one tribe to your son, for the sake of my servant David and for the sake of Jerusalem, which I have chosen.'"
(1 Kgs. 11:9 – 13)

There were in fact two tribes retained within Judah; the tribe of Judah and the reduced tribe of Benjamin (which was decimated at the time of the Judges (Jdgs. 19 – 21).

Although often treated as mere chattels by many of the ruling class, which is still evidenced in the middle east today, the wiles of women became well known because it was the only way they gained a voice.

By marrying girls from the surrounding pagan countries and by pandering to their need to worship their national gods rather than the God he should have worshipped and ensured they worshipped, Solomon gradually got dragged into worshipping their gods himself. Crucially, it was as mothers to his children that they would have ingrained into their children from birth when their brains were most receptive to the suggestion of the importance of the worship of their own tribal gods rather than the Lord God of Israel.

Solomon also did a great trade in horses with Egypt even though God had said through Moses:

- *he must not acquire many horses for himself, or go to Egypt to acquire more horses, since the Lord has said to you, 'You must never return that way again.'*

What God wanted as king was a man who lived simply and relied on Him as David had done, although even David had concubines, to not only give him wisdom to govern fairly but also to protect the land of Israel, which was not to say that he did not need troops capable of fighting, for in many instances the fighting could be fierce yet successful because God enabled them to win.

Sadly Solomon thought too hard and thought himself out of tune with God seeking the inspiration of other religions and got totally confused.

His son who succeeded him was Rehoboam who had been brought up surrounded by the luxurious opulence of the Court of King Solomon, acquiring many friends and hangers-on within the rich elite society of the day. He would have wanted for nothing.

However his mother was an Ammonite, one of the tribes God had told the Israelites they had to remove from the earth but did not do so, therefore God said that they would be a thorn in the nation's side, which was exactly what happened because there was constant war between Israel and the Ammonites. It was inevitable therefore that Rehoboam was taught by his mother about the Ammonite gods, not the God of Israel.

As he grew older, not only did King Solomon build altars to the gods worshipped by his various foreign wives, he also worshipped those gods himself. As the son of the only wife of Solomon that was referred to in scripture as having borne a child, it is clear that Rehoboam was not a proper Israelite, for a Jew is one who was born of a Jewish mother.

It is no wonder that growing up in the royal court Rehoboam was far removed from the ordinary families that suffered high taxes and labour call-ups to build great structures for the king, so that when he came to the throne of a united Israel he was impervious to the welfare concerns of the ordinary people.

Although, he had at his disposal old and young advisors, it was the advice of young, impetuous advisors that he favoured because, being inexperienced in real life issues and not as intimate with God as his father had been at the beginning, their advice was more in line with his own thinking.

If his father had oppressed the people then he would increase not decrease that oppression, after all he was not affected by the hard life they suffered. Solomon had been given a great deal of good advice before he became king. It does not seem that he passed on any advice to his son, who gives the appearance of being arrogant and hardhearted, which is so unlike his grandfather David.

In the account of Jeroboam, Rehoboam takes a back seat because, once he and his young advisors had made the mistake of being ignorant of the mood of the ordinary people of the ten tribes, the situation was out of his control.

Jeroboam, on the other hand, had a far more grounded upbringing. The son of a widowed mother, he had to fight to be educated and gain work and respect, which gave him a strong and independent character and probably a stubborn will which showed later when he became king. It was that independent character with a stubborn will that was ultimately the cause of his demise.

Being made king of the new Israel, Jeroboam did not seek the advice and direction of the God who appointed him but independently decided to prevent the people going to the temple in Jerusalem to worship God by providing two temples of golden calves who he claimed had brought the Israelites out of Egypt to the promised land in which they were living., the same god that Aaron cast whilst the Israelites were encamped at the base of Mount Sinai, and the same claim, which resulted in much slaughter.

This set the nation of Israel on a divergent course from their God with the result that there was instability in the country with kings not lasting very long and with foreign powers invading the country, so that it gradually disintegrated until the Assyrians took most of the people into exile, replacing them with people from other nations, this corrupted the purity of Israel which became known as the Samaritans, hence the hatred of them by Jews of Jesus' day. Even today it is not part of Israel.

As regards the people of Judah they did not fare much better for Rehoboam was succeeded by his son Abijah who was brought up worshipping Ammonite gods.

All the laws of God were written down for a very good reason. It is very difficult for many people to realize that the very first man was created by God according to His sovereign will and with the express purpose of him living in communion with God, in which state man would find peace and purpose. Sadly the rebellious nature of the Israelites, and the mixture that came out of Egypt, meant that they did not follow God's laws as they should have done and suffered as a result. All, that is, except for a remnant which stayed loyal to their God.

Abijah survived just three years when Asa came to the throne and what a breath of fresh air King Asa must have been to the devout Jews of his time, removing the hateful images and altars dedicated to all those gods of the surrounding nations that drew the population away from the worship of their own God YaWHeH (I Am Who I Am).

As soon as his father had died Asa wanted to rid the country of the worship of all foreign gods and to focus the attention of the population on the worship of the one true God. So he started the process of destroying all the effigies and altars dedicated to the foreign gods that had greatly multiplied throughout the kingdom of Judah because of Solomon's wives and the evil reign of his father Abijah.

Not only that but he encouraged the people to seek after the Lord their God and observe His laws and commandments, which brought peace to the nation. In Chronicles we read that during the first ten years of his reign there was no threat of war. This happened because the king encouraged the people to reach out to God, seeking Him as individuals so that the nation as a whole became God focused which enabled God to give them rest, as was promised through Moses.

Such was his determination to have his people turn to God, he even had his grandmother, the granddaughter of Absolom, David's rebellious son who cause his father much anguish and suffering, removed from her royal position of queen mother because of the obscene image of Asherah, the Canaanite goddess of fertility, she had made and placed in the Temple, which he destroyed by the brook Kidron.

Asa was not an ambitious king preferring to fortify the land to protect it from being invaded and to live in peace. He did raise an army of 580,000 men. However when he heard that Zerah of Ethiopia was approaching with a vast army that outnumbered his own army many times over and realizing his army was no match for the approaching army, Asa called on the name of God and it is very interesting what he said to God.

> *"It is nothing for you to help us, the powerless against the mighty. Help us O Lord for we trust in you alone and it is in your name that we face this vast horde. Please do not let mere men prevail against you."*

The Lord, in answering the king's prayer, took action and destroyed the army of Ethiopia.

There will have been much euphoria within the army as they were given the victory by God. So the Lord sent a prophet to them, Ahaziah son of Oded, to give them this warning:

> *The Lord is with you all the while you are with Him.*
> *If you seek Him, He will be found by you;*
> *but if you forsake Him, He will forsake you.*

This is the consistent message throughout scripture and it seems that it was one that the whole of Israel quickly forgot during times of peace when earthly distractions experienced during their daily lives drew them away from God.

It is interesting that Jehoshaphat took after his father Asa in not worshipping the Baals as Rehoboam and Abijah had done, but focused his attention on worshipping the God of Israel. However, the weakness of his father's character also had an effect on his own character.

There can be no doubt that children carry their parents genes and are deeply influenced by the actions of their parents during their formative years. Although it was very clear that his father Asa was completely different to his grandfather and great grandfather in that rather than worshipping pagan gods, he worshipped the God of Israel, there were flaws in his character and in his understanding of God and His requirements which caused him to err, such as his decision to hire the services of a potential adversary Ben-Hadad of Aram, rather than rely on God to deliver him from threats from Israel as He had done with the Ethiopian threat.

Faith and trust in God is not contagious, nor can it be passed down from parent to child or between siblings and friends, except perhaps by example, but there has to be the potential curiosity and willingness to search for and find God within the individual as can be seen in Jacob, for example.

Every individual human being must find God for themselves and then develop a trust in Him over time. It is as much a learning curve as learning about life and gaining knowledge of practical and scholarly things just like all previous generations.

What Asa had obviously not realized was that God wanted to be involved in every aspect of his reign, even the diplomatic and defensive strategies required to contain his neighbour Israel and keep his country safe.

Jehoshaphat had the same problem. Where the odds were clearly against him he called upon God's assistance, but for the more mundane and everyday decision making he believed he could do very well on his own. Sadly, as we all discover at some point, we are prone to making mistakes. For Asa it was to find out from God that by making his own arrangements with Ben-Hadad he missed a vital opportunity to rid himself of the potential danger of the Aramean army.

There is no doubt that the split up of the nation of Israel into two countries was something of a running sore with each part wanting control, or at least have influence over the other. With this in mind, and for political expediency, Jehoshaphat made the mistake of allowing his son and heir Jehoram to marry Athalia, the daughter of the weak king Ahab and the ruthlessly evil Jezebel. It was this mistake that was to cost the royal family of Judah very dear indeed.

All the while Jehoshaphat focused on the Lord, obeying His commandments and ensuring He was central to his life and the lives of his subjects, even sending his officials along with Levites and priests throughout the country teaching the people, God gave him peace because the fear of the Lord fell on all the surrounding nations preventing them from declaring war on Judah.

Instead of threats, gifts were brought to the king making him immensely rich and with him being held in high esteem he became more and more powerful.

But with the accession of Jehoram Judah fell into the same state as Israel under the evil Jezebel worshipping other gods. Thus from Jehoram's perspective he started to lose influence amongst the nations. The Edomites were the first to revolt and crown their own king, and even though the king tried to recover the situation through force of arms, the scriptures tell us that Edom has been independent of Judah to this day.

Elijah wrote a letter to Jehoram:

> *"The Lord, the God of your ancestor David, says: "You have not followed the good example of your father, Jehoshaphat, or your grandfather King Asa of Judah. Instead, you have been as evil as the kings of Israel. You have led the people of Jerusalem and Judah into harlotry through the worship of idols, just as King Ahab did in Israel. And you have even killed your own brothers, men who were better than you.*
> *Be warned that now the Lord is about to strike you, your people, your children, your wives, and all that is yours with a heavy blow. You will become very sick and suffer with a severe intestinal disease that will get worse each day until your bowels come out."*

Jehoram was now experiencing the wrath of God and because he was the perpetrator of the nation's rejection of God, he would suffer greatly.

After Jehoram's death his son Ahaziah ruled but he was killed by Jehu when visiting his parents-in-laws Ahab and Jezebel. So Athalia took the throne until after six years she was killed and Joash ascended the throne aged just seven.

What is very clear in all that was happening in Judah, which led to the people going into exile, was their increasingly fickle observance of the instructions and commandments of the Lord their God. Moses called upon the Israelites to choose between life and death; being obedient to and serving the Lord their God or abandoning Him. Finally God had had enough of them because they were continually being disobedient, therefore He was abandoning them, allowing the Babylonians to take them into exile which, according to Jeremiah, was to last seventy years.

7 GOD RESTORES HIS PEOPLE

No nation or ruler is too big for God to handle or for Him to use for His own ends. Judah had gone seriously wrong with the kings and priests openly defying Him, so He used Nebuchadnezzar and the Babylonian empire to judge the people of Judah by exiling them.

As part of His strategy for teaching the people why He had had them sent into exile he chose a priest by the name of Ezekiel to teach them all about their errors.

The kings were having the images of gods erected in the temple, and the priests were worshipping created things rather than the Lord their God. They were supposed to be priests of God not of man, and they were to be the intermediary between God and His people, opening up the word and interpreting it to the people, not worshipping the sun or creatures as Ezekiel discovered through a vision of what had been secretly happening in the temple buildings (Eze. 8).

The prophets Isaiah and Jeremiah both sought to warn the king and people about the impending disaster that awaited them if they did not turn back to God, but the prophets were ignored. Indeed the last king had all Jeremiah's writings destroyed so that Jeremiah, using hie secretary Baruch, had to rewrite all that he had previously written. God has a very good memory.

But Judah was the tribe in which the Messiah would be born so God, towards the end of the seventy years of exile as prophesied by Jeremiah, arranged for Nehemiah, a devout Jew, to receive news of the state of Jerusalem.

It came to pass in the month of Chislev, in the twentieth year, as I was in Shushan the citadel, that Hanani one of my brethren came with men from Judah; and I asked them concerning the Jews who had escaped, who had survived the captivity, and concerning Jerusalem. 3 And they told me, "The survivors who are left in the province are in great distress and reproach. The wall of Jerusalem is also broken down, and its gates are burned with fire."
So it was, when I heard these words, that I sat down and wept, and mourned for many days; I was fasting and praying before the God of heaven. (Neh. 1:1 – 4)

So Nehemiah prayed to the Lord God of heaven who keeps His

covenant and mercy with those who love You and observe Your commandments, 6 please let Your ear be attentive and Your eyes open, that You may hear the prayer of Your servant which I am praying before You now, day and night, for the children of Israel Your servants. I confess the sins of the children of Israel which we have sinned against You. Both my father's house and I have sinned. 7 We have acted very corruptly against You, and have not kept the commandments, the statutes, nor the ordinances which You commanded us to observe through Your servant Moses. (Neh. 1:5 – 7)

Nehemiah then reminded the Lord the word that He gave Moses

'If you are unfaithful and violate your obligations to Me I will scatter you among the nations; but if you return to Me and keep My commandments and do them, though those of you who have been scattered are in the remotest part of the heavens, I will gather you from there and will bring you to the place I have chosen for My Name to dwell.' (Neh. 1:8, 9)

He then asked for God to prosper him when he went before the king because being the king's cupbearer if he appeared downhearted he could be killed.

What are we to gain from this passage? That Nehemiah firstly showed remorse at the state of the place where God had place His great name, acknowledged the greatness of the Lord and confessed the sins of the fathers and his own sin. He then reminded the Lord of His promise to bring the scattered nation back to the land *if you return to Me and keep My commandments and do them.*

What this tells is that the Lord had the ability to re-establish the nation in its homeland providing there was a complete change of attitude towards Him, that the prophecy of Jeremih was perfectly correct for God knew all that would happen.

So Nehemiah went before the king and the king said to him *"Why is your face sad, since you are not sick? This is nothing but sorrow of heart."*

God was indeed blessing him with that remark from the King.

> *Why should my face not be sad, when the city, the place of my fathers' tombs, lies waste, and its gates are burned with fire?"*
> *Then the king said to me, "What do you request?"*
> *So praying to the God of heaven. I said to the king, "If it pleases the king, and if your servant has found favor in your sight, I ask that you send me to Judah, to the city of my fathers' tombs, that I may rebuild it."*
> *Then the king said to me, "How long will your journey be? And when will you return?" So it pleased the king to send me; and I set him a time.*
>
> (Neh. 2:3 – 6)

So with letters clearing his way to Jerusalem, and to cover the timber needed for the gates and for the house he would occupy, along with a contingent of the army to provide him with protection, clearly indicating that the Lord was with him, Nehemiah went to Jerusalem.

There he met with much opposition from those who had taken over the running of the city. But in the dead of night with just a few men with him he surveyed the damage to the walls and the gates. Only then did he reveal the purpose of his visit.

> *Then I said to them, "You see the distress that we are in, how Jerusalem lies waste, and its gates are burned with fire. Come and let us build the wall of Jerusalem, that we may no longer be a reproach." And I told them of the hand of my God which had been good upon me, and also of the king's words that he had spoken to*

me.
So they said, "Let us rise up and build." Then they set their hands to this good work.

(Neh.2:17, 18)

Key opposition figures ridiculed all their efforts, but Nehemiah prayed:

Hear, O God, for we are despised; turn their reproach on their own heads, and give them as plunder to a land of captivity! Do not cover their iniquity, and do not let their sin be blotted out from before You; for they have provoked You to anger before the builders.
So we built the wall, and the entire wall was joined together up to half its height, for the people had a mind to work.

(Neh. 4:4 – 6)

As they saw the work succeeding and the wall up to half its height, the opposition became very angry, conspiring together to attack the city and cause confusion, but prayer was made to almighty God and a watch was set against them day and night with armed men in the gaps so that the opposition was unsuccessful in frustrating the work.

Did you notice that not only was prayer made to almighty God but they took responsibility to protect themselves because God would empower them in their defense of the city.

Sadly only a few saw fit to return and suffer deprivations whilst working on the wall. Many stayed in the Babylonian empire having gained status within it, property and businesses. But those who did return were tested for genealogy.

It was now time for the reading of the Law by Ezra the scribe who had studied the law all the while he was in captivity and knew it intimately. With all the people gathered together he stood on a platform raised above the people and read the law all morning. Others were there to explain the law as it was being read, translating and explaining it.

Then Nehemiah, the governor, and Ezra the priest and scribe, and the Levites who taught the people said to all the people,
"This day is holy to the Lord your God;

do not mourn or weep."
For all the people were weeping when they heard the words of the
Law. Then Ezra said to them,

> *"Go your way, eat the rich festival food, drink the sweet*
> *drink, and send portions to him for whom nothing is*
> *prepared; for this day is holy to our Lord. And do not be*
> *sorrowful, for the joy of the Lord is your strength and your*
> *stronghold."*

So the Levites quieted all the people, saying, "Be still, for the day is
holy; do not be sorrowful."
Then all the people went on their way to eat, to drink, to send
portions of food to others and to celebrate a great festival, because
they understood the words which had been read to them.
(Neh. 8:9 – 12)

On the second day of the reading of the law as revealed by Moses was about the festival of booths, so the people went out and got material for building booths and celebrated the festival for the first time since the time Joshua was their leader. There was very great gladness. So from the first day until the last day Ezra read from the law the words of God to Moses.

The people committed themselves to live according to the Law of God and give their dues to the temple.

The Temple Rebuilt

Once the city walls were rebuilt and the city gates hung the people got to work on their houses forgetting all about the centrality of the worship of God in the temple to their faith in God. Many still remembered the glorious temple of Solomon and were fearful of erecting something far less grand and kept putting it off, but God had other ideas.

Haggai, prophet to the governor and high priest received a word from the Lord:

> *"Is it time for you yourselves to dwell in your paneled houses, and*
> *this temple to lie in ruins?" Now therefore, thus says the Lord of*
> *hosts: Consider your ways!*

"You have sown much, and bring in little;
You eat, but do not have enough;
You drink, but you are not filled with drink;
You clothe yourselves, but no one is warm;
And he who earns wages,
Those wages go into a bag with holes."

The temple and the worship services within it should have been central to their daily lives, yet they were putting off rebuilding it, preferring to look after their own comfort rather than biding by their responsibility to God to build Him a house that represented His presence amongst them.

Yet it was their God who had facilitated their return and the reading of the law. It was He who had kept them safe from those who would prevent them from rebuilding the city walls and hanging the gates. And here they were ignoring His house.

Thus says the Lord of hosts: "Consider your ways! Go up to the mountains and bring wood and build the temple, that I may take pleasure in it and be glorified," says the Lord.

They seemed never to have learned that in Egypt the river supplied all the field irrigation, but in this promised land they were dependent upon the Lord to provide the former and latter rains.

"You looked for much, but it came to little; and when you brought it home, I blew it away. Why?" says the Lord of hosts. "Because My house is in ruins, while every one of you runs to his own house.

God had to be central to their daily lives, to be consulted by kings and leaders of the people, to be part of their very existence. Had He not responded to the cry of Nehemiah and caused the king to be merciful to him and grant his request to restore the walls of Jerusalem? Had He not been with the various parties leaving Babylon and the surrounding area to protect them and restore to them their nation's lands? Why then were they so reluctant to restore the house of the Lord?

Therefore the heavens above you will withhold the dew, and the earth withholds its fruit. For I called for a drought on the land and the mountains, on the grain and the new wine and the oil, on whatever the ground brings forth, on men and livestock, and on all the labour of your hands."

(Hag. 1:4 – 11)

This just demonstrates the importance of the temple to the Lord which represented His dwelling place amongst them. With that challenge the people responded, led by Zerubbabel the governor and Joshua the high priest along with all the remnant of the people answering the words from the Lord given to them by Haggai the prophet. So they worked on the house of the Lord with a will.

Their activity pleased the Lord and He spoke again through his prophet Haggai saying, *"I am with you."*

Almost a month later the Lord asked them, *'Who is left among you who saw this temple in its former glory? And how do you see it now? Is this not nothing in your eyes in comparison?*

Yet now be strong, Zerubbabel,' says the Lord; 'and be strong, Joshua, son of Jehozadak, the high priest; and be strong, all you people of the land,' says the Lord, 'and work; for I am with you,' says the Lord of hosts. 'According to the word that I covenanted with you when you came out of Egypt, so My Spirit remains among you; so do not fear!' (Hag. 2:3 – 5)

Then the Lord comforts them further saying:

'The glory of this latter temple shall be greater than the former,' says the Lord of hosts. 'And in this place I will give peace,' says the Lord of hosts." (Hag. 2:9)

The new temple took just over four years to complete in spite of various attempts to delay or bring its construction to an end. Indeed a decree from Darius added to the original decree by Cyrus that every help be made available to the construction and running of the temple.

Cleansing the Priesthood

When Ezra arrived in Jerusalem he started to hear about the

contamination of the priesthood. How the Levites had not separated themselves from the people of the lands, from the abominations of the Canaanites, Hittites, Perizzites, Jebusites, Ammonites, Moabites, Egyptians and Amorites, but married into their families. So that their seed was mixed with the people's of those lands. In fact the leaders and rulers were foremost in this trespass.

Ezra was astonished and tore his clothes, sitting down in astonishment until the time of the evening sacrifice. He was joined by those who trembled at the words of the God of Israel sitting with him because of this outrage committed by the returning exiles.

So he prayer

> "O my God, I am too ashamed and humiliated to lift up my face to You, my God; for our iniquities have risen higher than our heads, and our guilt has grown up to the heavens.
> Since the days of our fathers to this day we have been very guilty, and for our iniquities we, our kings, and our priests have been delivered into the hand of the kings of the lands, to the sword, to captivity, to plunder, and to humiliation, as it is this day.
> And now for a little while grace has been shown from the Lord our God, to leave us a remnant to escape, and to give us a peg in His holy place, that our God may enlighten our eyes and give us a measure of revival in our bondage.
> For we were slaves. Yet our God did not forsake us in our bondage; but He extended mercy to us in the sight of the kings of Persia, to revive us, to repair the house of our God, to rebuild its ruins, and to give us a wall in Judah and Jerusalem.
> And now, O our God, what shall we say after this? For we have forsaken Your commandments, which You commanded by Your servants the prophets, saying, 'The land which you are entering to possess is an unclean land, with the uncleanness of the peoples of the lands, with their abominations which have filled it from one end to another with their impurity. (Ezra 9:6 – 11)

The sense of guilt and despair was clear in the wording of his prayer to God for mercy:

> And after all that has come upon us for our evil deeds and for our great guilt, since You our God have punished us less than our

iniquities deserve, and have given us such deliverance as this to survive as a remnant.

But here we are again breaking Your commandments, and join in marriage with the people committing these abominations? Would You not be angry with us until You had consumed us, so that there would be no remnant or survivor?

O Lord God of Israel, You are righteous and just, for we are left as a remnant, as it is this day. We come before You, in our guilt, though in such circumstances no one can stand before You!" (Ezra 9:13 – 15)

What a prayer in such circumstances. It is truly repentant and seeking the mercy of the Lord. But Ezra did not just seek forgiveness and mercy from the Lord, he did something about it. Whilst praying before the evening sacrifice, confessing and weeping and bowing down before the house of God, a very large assembly gathered weeping very bitterly.

Then one, Shechaniah by name. spoke up admitting:

"We have trespassed against our God, and have taken pagan wives from the peoples of the land; yet now there is hope in Israel in spite of this.

Now therefore, let us make a covenant with our God to put away all these wives and those who have been born to them, according to the advice of my master and of those who tremble at the commandment of our God; and let it be done according to the law.

Arise, for this matter is your responsibility. We also are with you. Be of good courage, and do it." (Ezra 10:2 – 4)

If ever there was a word from the Lord that was it, and Ezra reacted accordingly making the leaders of the priests, Levites and all Israel swear an oath to do according to this word. So they swore an oath.

Then there was a gathering of all the men of Judah and Benjamin in Jerusalem, sitting in the open square of the house of God trembling because of this matter of their sin before the Lord.

Then Ezra the priest stood up and said to them, "You have transgressed and have taken pagan wives, adding to the guilt of

Israel. Now therefore, make confession to the Lord God of your fathers, and do His will; separate yourselves from the peoples of the land, and from your pagan wives." (Ezra 10:10, 11).

Although they asked for time to sort this matter out because it was the time of heavy rain, they agreed to do what was asked so that *the fierce wrath of our God is turned away from us in this matter.*

As with the departure of Ishmael and his mother Hagar from Abraham, and Esau from Jacob, there are consequences. It is all very well all these men discarding their wives and offspring, but what it did was to generate animosity and resentment in the minds of those discarded which cause anguish and disruption for future generations.

They had transgressed and to remain loyal to God they had to separate themselves from their wives and offspring. But there were consequences for they were discarding real people with real feelings. What were these people to do for a home and financial support? Supposing they had nowhere else to go, no family to take them in?

No wonder there is such animosity towards the Jews today for memories are long in the middle east. Through their sin they had created problems for future generations.

They would certainly need God's protective hand.

8 THE PROMISE OF A MESSIAH

From the moment of Adam's sin God already had a plan in His mind to restore mankind to Himself and the first Messianic promise was given to Satan:

> *And I will put enmity*
> *Between you and the woman,*
> *And between your seed and her Seed;*
> *He shall bruise your head,*
> *And you shall bruise His heel."*
> *(Gen. 3:15)*

There was to be no love lost between Satan and his fallen angels and man, for the One that was to come would bruise his head, through His resurrection and ascension although Satan would bruise His heel by causing Him to die on the cross.

This animosity would fester and Satan would do all within his power to frustrate the work of God and be a constant impediment to the work of God through His chosen people, all the while allowing God to demonstrate His great and awesome power.

But scattered throughout scripture are little gems of truth regarding the coming of the Messiah and what sort of person He would be, for Jesus Himself referred to all scripture:

> *"How foolish you are, and how slow to believe all that the prophets*
> *have spoken! Was it not necessary for the Messiah to suffer these*

things and then enter his glory?' And beginning with Moses and all the Prophets, he explained and interpreted to them what was said in all the Scriptures concerning himself." (Luke 24:25-27).

It is not my intention to list all the references to the coming Messiah here because the object of this book is to show that God had a plan to deal with man from the beginning, knowing full well all that would happen, yet He still went ahead with the creation of man because, although the majority of men (including women) would reject Him, there would be a remnant consisting of those that would believe in Him. It would be such as those who would finally enter into His glorious rest.

It was His intense love of man that caused Him to deal with man from the beginning, at first choosing specific people and then a nation and within that nation specific people through whom He aimed to reach a great number of people throughout the world.

He established certain covenantal arrangements with individuals such a Noah and Abram, and with the chosen nation through Moses and David. But the Messiah would bring in a much greater covenant with those that believed in Him as their saviour, a covenant by which they would enjoy eternal life in His resting place.

"Behold, the days are coming," says the Lord, "when I will make a new covenant with the house of Israel (the Northern Kingdom) and with the house of Judah (the Southern Kingdom), but not like the covenant I made with their fathers in the day when I took them by the hand to bring them out of the land of Egypt, My covenant which they broke, although I was a husband to them," says the Lord.
"But this is the covenant which I will make with the whole house of Israel after those days," says the Lord, "I will put My law within them, I will write it on their hearts; and I will be their God, and they will be My people.
And each man will no longer teach his neighbor and his brother, saying, 'Know the Lord,' for they will all know Me through personal experience, from the least of them to the greatest," says the Lord. "For I will forgive their wickedness, and I will no longer remember their sin." (Jer. 31:31 – 34)

There is one member of the Godhead who has been consistently working in the world and He is the Holy Spirit. From hovering over the waters at the very beginning, causing the flood that saved Noah and the miraculous events in Egypt that led to the Pharaoh releasing the people, and earthquakes and drought. The Holy Spirit is the power of God on and in the earth throughout the history of the earth.

Jesus is described as the Word of God, but it was the Holy Spirit who implanted knowledge into the minds of the prophets causing them to write down the words they were given by the Holy Spirit. What has become our Bible. As Paul wrote to Timothy:

> *All Scripture is God-breathed, given by inspiration of the Holy Spirit, and is profitable for instruction, for conviction of sin, for correction of error and restoration to obedience, for training in learning to live in conformity to God's will, both publicly and privately; so that the man of God may be complete, proficient, and thoroughly equipped for every good work. (2 Tim. 3:16, 17)*

And Peter

> *So we have the prophetic word made confirmed. You do well to pay close attention to it as to a lamp shining in a dark place, until the day dawns and light breaks through and the morning star arises in your hearts.*
> *First of all knowing that no prophecy of Scripture is a matter of or comes from one's own personal or special interpretation, for no prophecy was ever made by an act of human will, but men moved by the Holy Spirit spoke from God. (2 Peter 1:19 – 21)*

The Holy Spirit was very restricted up to the time of the appearance of the Messiah when He worked in conjunction with the Word made flesh, causing things to happen as instructed by the Word of God.

It was after the ascension of the Son of God who was made flesh that He gained much greater freedom to act amongst those that have been saved by the blood of the Lamb. Indeed it is He who applies the cleansing blood to truly repentant individuals.

It is also He who brings the word to life in the minds of true believers. The Lord Jesus when talking to the disciples told them that there was much more that He wanted to tell them, to teach them but they were in no fit state to hear it at that time, however when He sent the Holy Spirit to them it was He who would guide them into all truth for He would speak all that He heard from the Lord Jesus

> *and He will disclose to you what is to come. He will glorify and honor Me, because the Holy Spirit will take from what is Mine and will disclose it to you. All things that the Father has are Mine. Because of this I said that the Spirit will take from what is Mine and will reveal it to you. (John 16:13 – 15)*

The new covenant in His blood, to all those who are fully repentant and seek to embed themselves in and fully associate themselves with Christ Jesus, will cause the Holy Spirit to become part of them thus *each man will no longer teach his neighbor and his brother, saying, 'Know the Lord,' for they will all know Me through personal experience, from the least of them to the greatest.*

It is clear that all that happened to the Messiah was recorded in scripture well before He arrived on the earth to pursue His ministry. For consider Psalm 22:

> *1 My God, My God, why have You forsaken Me?*
> *Why are You so far from helping Me,*
> *And from the words of My groaning?*

The Lord's cry from the cross (Matt. 27:46)

> *And about the ninth hour Jesus cried out with a loud voice, saying, "Eli, Eli, lama sabachthani?" that is, "My God, My God, why have You forsaken Me?"*

> *8 "He trusted in the Lord, let Him rescue Him;*
> *Let Him deliver Him, since He delights in Him!"*

The comment of those who watched Him (Matt. 27:43)

> *He trusted in God; let Him deliver Him now if He will have Him; for He said, 'I am the Son of God.' "*

But that was not to be for He hung on the cross not because of His own sin, because He was sinless, but for the sins of all men past, present and future.

> *18 They divide My garments among them,*
> *And for My clothing they cast lots.*

That is what the soldiers did (Matt: 27:35).

> *Then they crucified Him, and divided His garments, casting lots, that it might be fulfilled which was spoken by the prophet:*
> *"They divided My garments among them,*
> *And for My clothing they cast lots."*

According to the angel Gabriel the Messiah would come according to a timetable, for Daniel was told that seventy sevens, 490 years would pass climaxing not merely in the return from Babylon but in the age of the anointed One, or Messiah. What an encouragement that must have been to Daniel!

> *"Seventy weeks are decreed about your people and your holy city,* **to finish the transgression, to put an end to sin, and to atone for iniquity, to bring in everlasting righteousness, to seal both vision and prophet, and to anoint the Most Holy.**

This must refer to (in Old Testament language) the Anointed One, or in New Testament language, the Messiah, for He was responsible for doing all those things:

to finish the transgression — meaning to bring it to fulfilment. There are two passages that give clarity to this statement.

In Genesis 15:16, God tells Abraham that after enduring slavery in Egypt, his descendants will return to the promised land, *"for the iniquity of the Amorites is not yet complete."*

Regarding the sin of Jesus' generation, He said to the religious leaders of the Jews that *"on you may come all the righteous blood shed on earth, from the blood of righteous Abel to the blood of Zechariah the son of Barachiah, whom you murdered between the sanctuary and the altar. Truly, I say to you, all these things will come upon this generation" (Matthew 23:35, 36).*

Rabbinic teaching indicated that the destruction of the Temple came about because of the sins of the previous generation. God takes action at such a point. But in destroying the Temple in which animals were used as substitutes for the people, God also graciously provided a means of atonement without the Temple — the atoning death of Jesus through whose shed blood we can be saved from the penalty of death.

This meant that the Holy Spirit no longer dwelt in physical buildings made through the efforts of men, but in living human beings.

to put an end to sin — suggests that the Messiah atones for our sin. To the Romans Paul wrote, *"God shows his love for us in that while we were still sinners, Christ died for us. Because if while we were enemies we were reconciled to God by the death of his Son, how much more, now that we are reconciled, shall we be saved by his life." (Ro. 5:8, 10).* Not only was he resurrected, but He also ascended to be our advocate on high.

to atone for iniquity — at the final Passover meal Jesus so desired to celebrate with His disciples, He took the cup, the third cup of the Seder representing redemption, and when He had given thanks He gave it to them saying, *'Drink of it, all of you, for this is my blood of the new covenant, which is poured out for you and for many for the forgiveness of sins.'"* (Matt. 26:27-28)

to bring in everlasting righteousness — this has been made possible because, as Paul says in Romans 5:17, *'For if, because of one man's trespass [that of Adam], death reigned through that one man, how much more will those who receive the abundance of grace and the free gift of righteousness reign in life through the one man Messiah Jesus."*

In other words, as we are cleansed, through repentance and faith in Jesus, by His shed blood, so in living a life committed to Him in order that we might serve Him, we receive the abundance of grace because he was victorious over the death penalty imposed by the Father and is even now living in the presence of His Father in heaven.

to seal both vision and prophet — This can mean one of two things. Either:

to authenticate something, which Jesus certainly did regarding the words of the prophets concerning his life, death and resurrection. But it was He as the Word of the Father who gave them the words to say, thus He was fulfilling His own prophetic word.

Or

to hide the meaning of Scripture from those who reject him. To the disciples Jesus said: *"To you it has been given to know the mysteries of the kingdom of God, but to the rest it is given in parables, that*
'Seeing they may not see,
And hearing they may not understand.'

There was an openness amongst the disciples to know the things of God, but to the religious leaders of the Jews there was no such desire, so full of their own importance were they. This reflected something God told Isaiah:

> *9And He said, "Go, and tell this people:*
> *'Keep on hearing, but do not understand;*
> *Keep on seeing, but do not perceive.'*
> *10"Make the heart of this people dull,*
> *And their ears heavy,*
> *And shut their eyes;*
> *Lest they see with their eyes,*
> *And hear with their ears,*
> *And understand with their heart,*
> *And return and be healed."*
> *(Is. 6:9, 10)*

This is cynicism, but truth because the people's hearts had become hardened to the words of God beyond repentance. But why did God send Isaiah out to preach?

> *11 Then I said, "Lord, how long?"*
> *And He answered:*
> *"Until the cities are laid waste*
> *and without inhabitant,*
> *The houses are without a man,*
> *The land is utterly desolate,*
> *12 The Lord has removed men far away,*
> *And the forsaken places are many*
> *in the midst of the land.*
> *13 But yet even if a tenth survive,*
> *The invader will return and destroy.*
> *But as a terebinth tree or as an oak*
> *Whose stump remains when it is cut down.*
> *So the stump of Israel will be a holy seed."*
> *(Is. 6:11 – 13)*

Israel had come to the end of the line with regard to God's patience and both Israel and Judah would be sent into exile. But with Israel, they would be absorbed into the Assyrian empire and disappear, although God would know who the faithful were and never lose sight of them.

For Judah there was a sufficient number of the remnant, such as Ezekiel and Daniel, who would keep the faith alive and one day return, but to a much reduced promised land. The stump from which would sprout new shoots.

to anoint the Most Holy — to anoint or consecrate the most holy place after its desecration, but, thinking about what the Lord said about the temple, *"Destroy this temple and in three days I will build it up."* He was talking about the temple that was His body. It is only when sin is at an end that God's presence can be perfectly manifested in the lives of individuals.

So we have the Saviour tabernacled amongst us and yet so many of those whose business it was to study the scriptures failed to recognize Him. Indeed they opposed Him in every way they could.

9 A SHORT HISTORY OF ISRAEL

There have been a number of significant points in the history of Israel when faith in God was in the ascendency. In a world of pagan worship there was a glimmer of light in Abram's acceptance of the God of creation as his Lord. This light lead through Isaac to Jacob who was searching for God and eventually found Him when wrestling with the angel on the mountain.

That light was picked up by Joseph whose life reflected that of the Messiah in that he was hated by his brothers because he was favoured by his father, sold into slavery of Gentiles, experienced a downturn in his fortunes by being placed in a dungeon before being elevated to the high place in Egypt by God, second only to the Pharaoh.

His initial steady decline in Egypt, even though he showed considerable skill in causing his first master to benefit financially, started with a woman who wanted something from him that he was not prepared to give. But in sending him to prison, God was putting him in a position where he could demonstrate spiritual skills in interpreting dreams to a contact with links to the Pharaoh. What is also clear is that Joseph's faith in God was undiminished no matter what his physical situation was.

Although it was possibly two years after his release that the butler revealed Joseph's name to the Pharaoh, it was according to God's timing for it was then that God alerted the Pharaoh to the impending famine, and the only one who could save the population from disaster was the God focused Joseph.

His sudden rise to power did not alter the character of Joseph even though all citizens had to bow low whenever he passed them. Indeed it was his lack of bitterness towards his brothers that was so evident in his treatment of them when they came seeking grain. How he gently taught them how cruel they had been to him but that God meant it for good in that he not only saved the people of Egypt and them from starvation but many others in the surrounding nations.

The Messiah went through similar experiences and was cruelly tormented and killed yet came out of it all victorious so that not only many Jews were saved from eternal death but also Gentiles of the surrounding nations.

The next light to shine brightly after many generations came from those who never lost faith in their God. The family of Moses were loyal to the God of their fathers, and Moses was chosen of God and put through a training programme that would enable him to lead the people out of slavery and to the land God had promised to Abraham.

Indeed given the edict passed by the Pharaoh that all Hebrew boys were to be killed at birth, Moses received training in the camp of the enemy which gave him the necessary training in leadership and the skill of dealing with the royal family that was to prove so imperative and successful later on.

His psychological fight with the Pharaoh in seeking to have his people released was significant because through him God was able to demonstrate His power over all the gods and goddesses then worshipped in Egypt, including the error that the Pharaoh was a god not a man.

In the process God set in motion a festival that would bring about the eternal salvation of millions of people worldwide. For the Son of God was sacrificed on the exact day set by God for the first Passover thousands of years later, in order to free us from our sinful entrapment by the attractions of the world.

The Passover meal was the beginning of the end of their entrapment in Egypt, and it was to protect the first-born of Israel from the angel of death who took away the lives of all the first-born from among the Egyptians and the other nations within the country that had not daubed the door posts and lintel with the blood of a sacrificed lamb. This was primarily aimed at the first-born of the Pharaoh who would have succeeded to the throne of Egypt on the death of his father.

The death of the Pharaoh when chasing after the people was

necessary because of his own free will he refused to give freedom to the children of Israel, thus they were still under his jurisdiction. As soon as he died they were freed legally from his control[8].

Moses led them the long way to the promised land because God wanted to mould them into a cohesive whole and purge from amongst the people those who had escaped with them but had no intention of abiding by the rules and laws of God. Many purgings of the people were necessary to cleanse them of the rebellious members.

Although Joshua was chosen of God to lead the people in the task to possess the land, he did not have the same charisma of Moses and when he died there was no successor so the whole of the promised land, which had not been fully conquered as God had required, fell to pieces. He left no organizational structure, and each of the tribes went their own way, except when the whole country was threatened by invaders or bandits.

At such times, after forgetting all about the Lord and their marriage to Him on Mount Sinai, God appointed a judge to rule over them for a period before the people returned to their old ways of ignoring Him. This was something that would plague the people throughout their pre-Messianic history and beyond to the present day.

Through the bareness of a wife pleading with God for a child came Samuel. Hannah was the barren wife of Elkanah suffering because his second wife had children. Promising to give the child she bore to Him to service in the tabernacle, God granted her wish and she was delivered of a boy child whom she named Samuel. He eventually became the high priest, in succession to Eli who died, and truly dedicated to God, serving Him well.

But again, just like the sons of Jacob, the sons of Samuel despoiled the temple with corrupt practices such that the people wanted a king to rule over them, not accepting that just as the offspring of their dedicated high priests went astray, so would the offspring of a king.

Saul was selected as king but his faith in God was weak and he failed various tests God put upon him.

God's next choice of king was a young boy called David, the

---

[8] When Jacob arrived in Egypt he agreed to come under the authority of the Pharaoh. For them to leave his authority the Pharaoh had to give his approval, which the Pharaoh was not prepared to do. By causing his death, God removed the Pharaoh and his heir. Thus by removing hose with authority over His people He legally freed His people.

youngest son of Jesse a Bethlehemite. He excelled as a leader of men and made Israel great. Although he failed God from time to time He loved God and God gave him fame and riches, uniting the whole of Israel.

Then came Solomon who started very well but then succumbed to the result of his disobeying the rules for kings laid out by Moses. He married women and had concubines from pagan nations who swayed him and caused him to worship their gods.

The account of Israel from there on became very bleak resulting in exile and inhabiting a diminishing land area of the promised land. But worse was to come for the priests continued to fail the people. Although they were priest of God who were the intermediaries between God and the people and should have been the ones who kept the people loyal to the God the nation married on Mount Sinai, they kept going astray.

This is what Isaiah (1) wrote:

Alas, O sinful nation,
A people laden down with iniquity,
A brood of evildoers,
Children who are corrupters!
They have forsaken the Lord,
They have provoked to anger
The Holy One of Israel,
They have turned away backward.
(Is. 1:4)

This nation through which God wanted to reach out to the world was in dire need of salvation, of commitment to their God.

Your country is desolate,
Your cities are burned with fire;
Foreigners plunder your fields in front of you;
Destroying everything they see.
So the daughter of Zion is left
as a booth in a vineyard,
As a hut in a garden of cucumbers,
As a besieged city.
If the Lord of the armies of heavens

Had not left to us a very small remnant,
We would have been wiped like Sodom,
We would have been destroyed like Gomorrah.
(Is. 1:7 – 9)

It seems the people had not learned from their history. It was back to the time of the judges. The problem was the lack of the sincerity of their hearts when offering their sacrifices. *What is the point of your sacrifices?* Asks the Lord. He had become sick of them because their life style did not reflect a life dedicated to Him or His service.

"Wash yourselves, make yourselves clean;
Put away the evil of your doings from before My eyes.
Cease to do evil, and learn to do good;
Seek justice, rebuke the oppressor;
Defend the fatherless, plead for the widow.
"Come now, and let us reason together,"
Says the Lord,
"Though your sins are like scarlet,
I will make them as white as snow;
Though they are red like crimson,
They shall be as wool.
(Is. 1:16, 17)

Then comes the challenge to come into a true relationship with their God and what would happen if they refused, and just continued on their disastrous way.

If you are willing and obedient,
You shall eat the good of the land;
But if you refuse and rebel,
You shall be devoured by the sword";
For the mouth of the Lord has spoken.
(Is. 1:19, 20)

Sadly they did nothing about the situation and suffered as a result, being sent into exile. Even after returning from exile, the people lasted for a time worshipping in the new temple and being obedient to the word of God, but then they reverted to the old ways yet again.

Isaiah was not the only one to criticize the population regarding their offerings. After the return from exile and the continued dominance of Persia, in spite of the people being able to return to their own land, the less than glorious temple and the need to purify themselves and discard pagan wives and children born to them, their obedience to the laws and instructions of Moses were not very strict and there was an element of not giving up on the gods they came to worship in Babylon.

Malachi weighed in on the work of the priests of God who were not following the laws of Moses. There is a statement and answer dialogue where God tells them that He loved them and they answer, *"in what way have you loved us?"* God replies, by you being the chosen, for Jacob, I loved and Esau I did not love.

"A son honors his father,
And a servant his master.
If then I am the Father,
Where is My honor?
And if I am a Master,
Where is My reverence?
Says the Lord of hosts
(Mal. 1:6)

God had not only created them but chose their nation to be His special people through whom He would reach out to the Gentile nations, but their basic desire to be no different to other nations became a major problem for God and a major obstacle to their progress in serving God.

They were blessed, and even when they went astray, as soon as they realized the error of their ways they returned to God He received them back and blessed them.

But the underlying insincerity of the priests and the people caused them to sin again and again as Malachi said:

To you priests who despise My name.
You say, 'In what way have we despised Your name?'
"You have shown contempt for my altar
By offering defiled food on it,
But you say,

'In what way have we defiled Your altar?'
By saying,
'The table of the Lord deserves no respect.'
(Mal. 1:end of 6, 7)

The requirements for the sacrificing of animals was that they had to be prefect in every way, representing a sinless animal, which was symbolic of the purity of the sacrifice of the Lamb of God many years later. From the point of view of the offeror, if he offered an imperfect animal that was one that he could not sell for profit and the priests turned a blind eye to it, instead of insisting that only perfect animals were sacrificed he would benefit financially for it cost him nothing, but as a meaningful sacrifice it was worth nothing.

Yet David when offered the threshing floor and oxen as a gift would not accept it saying *"No, but I will surely buy it for the full price, for I will not take what is yours for the Lord, nor offer burnt offerings with that which costs me nothing." (see 1 Chron. 21:18 – 28)*

But what was the point in seeking forgiveness for a sin and offering defective animals? Surely that meant they were only going through the motions of seeking forgiveness, that they did not really believe in God? They had no real respect for Him.

When you offer the blind animals as a sacrifice,
Is it not evil?
And when you offer the lame and sick,
Is it not evil?

We are referring to God the creator and sustainer of all that exists including man. We are in His debt; not Him indebted to us. If we treat Him with disrespect then our sins remain and we are in opposition to all that is of God.

God rightly gave an example of how serious the way they were treating Him was:

Offer those animals to your governor!
Would he be pleased with you?
Would he accept you favorably?"
Says the Lord of hosts.
(Mal. 1:8)

What this was actually doing was to besmirch His great name because they could not defend their land and were the laughing stock of the surrounding nations. How could they showcase his loving care of them? Or demonstrate the blessings with which He wanted to shower them?

> *Go ahead and beg God,*
> *That He may be gracious to us.*
> *While this is being done by your hands,*
> *Will He accept you favorably?"*
> *Says the Lord of hosts.*

When the Messiah came to the earth He was of the purest kind. From heaven He came to receive the body being prepared in the womb of a virgin, uncontaminated by the involvement of sinful man, thus was the Lamb of God entirely pure. He then sacrificed Himself on the cross for our sins.

The sacrifices on the altar were to be equally as pure for the forgiveness of sin, but by offering other than perfect animals there was no forgiveness, at all.

> *"Who is there among you who would shut the temple doors,*
> *So that these worthless offerings could not be offered?*
> *I have no pleasure in you,"*
> *Says the Lord of hosts,*
> *"Nor will I accept an offering from your hands.*

The priests were all corrupt and could no longer call themselves priests of God. Certainly as a missionary nation they were a complete failure.

> *For from the rising of the sun, even to its going down,*
> *My name shall be great among the Gentiles;*
> *In every place incense shall be offered to My name,*
> *And a pure offering;*
> *For My name shall be great among the nations,"*
> *Says the Lord of hosts.*
> *"But you profane it,*

In that you say,
'The table of the Lord is defiled;
And its fruit, its food, is contemptible.'
(Mal. 1:11, 12)

From the time of Adam and Eve through all their struggles all the Lord wanted to do was to glorify His name through them and lead many people into an intimacy with Him that would transform their lives, but they were doing the opposite.

As a nation they were a thorn in His side, causing harm to His great name. If it had not been for the remnant He would have abandoned them.

"For you bring the stolen, the lame, and the sick;
Thus you bring an offering!
Should I accept this from your hand?"
Says the Lord.
(Mal. 1:13b)

Such offerings did not go well for them, indeed they might just as well not offer a sacrifice at all for:

cursed be the deceiver
Who has in his flock a male,
And takes a vow,
But sacrifices to the Lord what is blemished

For I am a great King,"
Says the Lord of hosts,
"And My name is to be feared among the nations.
(Mal. 1:14)

Sadly the church is doing the same in that erroneous teaching is being preached and the sincerity of heart that is necessary when taking communion is not there. Will God deal graciously with us? For surely we are offering suspect sacrifices on the altar just as the priests did.

It is no wonder that God gave up on them and remained silent for four hundred years, during which time the situation merely got worse. For when the Messiah arrived the religious elite were so far removed from God that they effectively had their own brand of religion.

Certainly those who should have recognized the arrival of the Son of God were none the wiser when He began preaching, and they opposed Him.

10 THE ANOINTED ONE

The greatest miracle of all and one that speaks the loudest about the creator God was not only the coming of the Son of God to the earth but the manner in which it happened.

The Trinity is made up of three independent yet interdependent individuals of Father, Son and Spirit, all of whom have never been born and can never die. They live in the purest heaven so that sin is abhorrent to them.

The Father is the senior for it is He who decided to create the universe and the world, in which man was placed, alongside a spiritual world of angels with a hierarchy of Archangels and others.

The Son is the spokesman for the Father, for it is He who speaks the words of the Father. He is The Word.

The Spirit is the one who causes what the Son says to come into being. It is He who hovered over the waters on the embryonic earth, and it was He who was responsible for creating all that we see around us according to the thoughts of the Father as spoken by the Son.

The Son gave us the information when He said that He was about His Fathers business. Thus each one knows their place within the Trinity and are united in their roles within it.

From the beginning the Son was agreeable to becoming the all-sufficient sacrifice to save as many of mankind as possible from the second death. that is why all the sacrificial animals had to be pure in every respect for he is purity itself.

Coming to the earth as He did was a miracle, From being omnipresent, He was willing to enter into the embryo of a boy child in the womb of a virgin. As Charles Wesley put it:

Our God contracted to a span
Incomprehensively made man

This means that He acquired a human body which meant that He was not only the Son of God but also the Son of Man. However He retained the position of God because He could not be other than God, but by becoming first a child He became totally dependent upon the Holy Spirit and His human parents to protect Him.

The manner of his arrival is worth considering because God did it His way in that no humans were involved, not even the renting of a room in which He could be born. Rather a stable which provided the family with shelter. Also we have no teaching about when during the year He arrived on the earth; it is a mystery.

He was born in the city of David because his mother was of the lineage of David, as also was His step-father, which was important for His role in becoming the spiritual king of Israel in the line of David.

As witnesses to His birth were three Gentile men, astrologers from somewhere in the east, although how far they had to travel is unknown. And some low caste shepherds looking after their sheep nearby. But what is worth noting is that the religious elite, when called to advise King Herod as to where the Messiah was to be born, showed no curiosity as to why he was asking that question. They just gave the answer and left.

And, although the shepherds broadcast the news about the angels and seeing the young child, no one seemed to have been at all interested and the whole event was forgotten about, apart from remaining in the memories of those involved. So the arrival of the Son of God as the Son of Man was done in great secrecy, meaning that no scholar knew about Him or that He was the Son of God.

When it came time to dedicate the child and present Him to His Father at the temple, Simeon and Anna realized exactly who He was but those events were also of no public interest.

God then protected Himself by sending the parents with the child to Egypt until the death of Herod so that it was said, *Out of Egypt I called my Son.* What is particularly interesting is the ability of God to be one and yet for each member to go their own way and do their own work and yet continue to be totally united as one, each totally dependent upon the other two in a unity that is unbreakable. Only the Father never leaves heaven.

As proof that the Son of God, now named Jesus[9], was still part of God, when His body was twelve years old He was discovered in the temple discussing deep theology with scholars who were all amazed at His knowledge of scripture; but He was the cause of it being written. Also when his parents found Him He said to them *"Why did you seek Me? Did you not know that I must be about my Father's business?"* but they did not understand what He said to them.

The Lord submitted Himself to His human parents until He was thirty when He started his ministry.

Born six months before the Lord, John the Baptizer started his ministry of announcing the coming of the Messiah, separating himself from his priestly roots by living in the wilderness, away from habitation. His ministry struck a chord with the population for, with his disciples, he baptized many people.

> *Now this is the testimony of John,*
> *when the Jews sent priests and Levites from Jerusalem*
> *to ask him, "Who are you?"*
> *He did not deny, but confessed, "I am not the Christ."*
> *And they asked him, "What then? Are you Elijah?"*
> *He said, "I am not."*
> *"Are you the Prophet?"*
> *(Jn. 1:9 – 21)*

The prophet was mentioned by Moses who told the people to look out for one like him to whom they should listen .

> *And he answered, "No."*
> *Then they said to him, "Who are you,*
> *that we may give an answer*
> *to those who sent us?*

---

[9] Jesus' name in Hebrew is Yehoshua (Yeh-HO-shoo-ah), which, over time, became contracted to the shorter Yeshua (Yeh-SHOO-ah). Yehoshua, and therefore Yeshua as well, means "the Lord is salvation." This was turned into 'Jesus' in the English translations.

What do you say about yourself?"
He said: "I am
The voice of one crying in the wilderness:
"Make straight the way of the Lord," '
as the prophet Isaiah said."
Now those who were sent were from the Pharisees
Who asked him, "Why then do you baptize
if you are not the Christ, nor Elijah, nor the Prophet?"
John answered them, saying,
"I baptize with water, but there stands
One among you whom you do not know,
it is He who baptizes with the Holy Spirit.
He comes after me, but is preferred before me,
whose sandal strap I am not worthy to loose."
(Jn. 1:22 – 26)

In saying *but is preferred before me* John was acknowledging the superiority of the Son of God without actually naming Him.

Throughout the Lord's ministry, He was talking in spiritual terms of which the priests and Pharisees had no knowledge. Nicodemus, a leader of the Jews and a member of the supreme council of the Jews called the Sanhedrin, came to see the Lord at night so that it was in secret.

When Jesus told him that he had to be born again, he did not have a clue as to what He was talking about. Jesus had to explain that there is a physical world and a spiritual world. You are naturally born into one but need to be born into the other by a different process.

Jesus answered, "I assure you, unless one is born of water and the Spirit he cannot enter the kingdom of God.
That which is born of the flesh is flesh, and that which is born of the Spirit is spirit.

(Jn. 3:5, 6)

unless one is born of water could mean either human birth or the act of cleansing or purifying in running water as was required before certain rituals in the temple. What the Lord was seeking to tell Nicodemus was that there is a distinct separation between what we do as human beings and what happens in spiritual terms.

It is the Holy Spirit who makes us alive from a spiritual point of view in order for us to be able to speak to God and understand the things of God. This was the major problem for the priests and Pharisees, because they were cut off from God as they were dead from a spiritual point of view.

> *Do not be surprised that I have told you, 'You must be born again.'*
> *The wind blows where it wishes and you hear its sound, but you do*
> *not know where it is coming from and where it is going; so it is with*
> *everyone who is born of the Spirit."*
> *(Jn. 3:7, 8)*

The things of the Spirit cannot be discerned with human thinking, it is a totally different language, and just as we cannot see the wind or see where it starts or its destination, so are things of the Spirit

> *If I have told you earthly things and you do not believe, how will you*
> *believe if I tell you heavenly things?*
> *(Jn. 3:12)*

There are certain aspect of the Jewish faith that Nicodemus could not understand such as the true relationship between man and God. The giving of the ten commandments on Mount Sinai and the fact that it was on that mountain that Israel was married to God was an earthly truth with a spiritual dimension for how was Israel married to God?

It was a phenomenon that was hard to understand by those of a spiritual mind, but impossible for everyone else, particularly Nicodemus in his current spiritual and mental state.

> *No one has ascended to heaven but He who came down from*
> *heaven, that is, the Son of Man who is in heaven.*
> *(Jn. 3:13)*

The perfect knowledge of God is not obtained by anyone ascending to heaven, for that is the task of the Holy Spirit speaking to those who are open to the voice of God such as Abraham and Moses. But in taking on human flesh as *Son of Man*, He who was from everlasting came down to reveal His knowledge of the Father whom He knows intimately because of His eternal connection to heaven.

> *And as Moses lifted up the serpent in the wilderness, even so must the Son of Man be lifted up,*
>
> (Jn. 3:14)

The Lord knew why He had come and all that would happen to Him during His time on the earth. Here He is using the event in the wilderness when God told Moses to make an effigy of a serpent and put it on a pole so that anyone who had been bitten could look upon the effigy and be prevented from dying from the poison inflicted through their bite.

The Lord was made sin for us even though He was sinless. And just as those who looked upon the effigy of that serpent had to believe in its healing properties, so those sinner who want to be free of the condemnation of sin must believe in the efficacy of the blood shed by the Lord on the cross to cleanse them from sin.

> *that whoever believes in Him should not perish but have eternal life.*
>
> (Jn. 3:16b)

For God so loved the world tells us about the eternal love of the Father for the man He created and His desire that no one should perish. Although it was the Father who condemned man, it was His amazing Agape love that created the antidote to that condemnation.

> *For God so loved the world that He gave His only begotten Son, that whoever believes in Him should not perish but have everlasting life.*
>
> (Jn. 3:16)

Belief leading to repentance and commitment must precede the offer of everlasting life. And it was the Son who gave voice to the desire of the Father in giving His Son to suffer and die to provide salvation to any and all those that believe in Him.

> *For God did not send His Son into the world to condemn the world, but that the world through Him might be saved.*

(Jn. 3:17)

As Paul wrote to the Romans: *There is therefore now no condemnation to those who are in Christ Jesus, who do not walk according to the flesh, but according to the Spirit.*

That is the criteria. The degree of believing in the Lord Jesus Christ as Lord and Saviour. For to be 'in Christ' means to be filled with the Holy Spirit and fully committed to Him in heart, mind, soul and strength.

The seal of approval of the sacrificial death of the Messiah is given in the last supper He had with His disciples.

> *When the hour had come, He sat down, and the twelve apostles with Him. And He said to them, "I have fervently desired to eat this Passover with you before I suffer; for I say to you, I will no longer eat of it until it is fulfilled in the kingdom of God."*
> *(Lk. 22:14 – 16)*

This was the transition from the celebration of the Passover and celebrating his death until He returns. The ending of the remembrance of the last day in Egypt when a lamb was slain and the blood daubed on the door posts and lintel of the entrance to their homes leaving the first born safe inside as the angel of death went throughout the country, and the time of its fulfilment in the final sacrifice for sin when the Lamb of God was nailed to the tree in place of all men who had sinned against God, suffering agonizing pain for six hours with the last three being alone, without the Father. The first and last time they were ever separated from each other in all eternity.

First was His body that suffered greatly at the hand of the soldiers and then being nail to the cross:

> *He took bread, gave thanks, broke it, and gave it to them, saying, "This is My body which is given for you; do this in remembrance of Me."*
> *(Lk. 22:19)*

It is the blood that saves when it is applied to our personal account before God by the Spirit of God. Because blood is representative of the life blood of any living being and was precious in God's eyes.

> *Likewise He took the cup after supper, saying, "This cup is the new covenant in My blood, which is shed for you and for many for the remission of sins.*
>
> *(Lk. 22:14 – 16)*

But there is more to this than is recorded here for in the book of Hebrews we read:

> *For if the sprinkling of ceremonial defiled people with the blood of bulls and goats and the ashes of a heifer, sanctifies for the purifying of the flesh,*
>
> *(Heb. 9:13)*

This was a physical cleansing of the flesh of individuals in previous ceremonies, but did nothing for the inner man,

> *how much more shall the blood of Christ, who through the eternal Spirit*
>
> *(Heb. 9:14)*

For it was the Spirit of God who was the witness to the sacrifice and it is He who applies the blood to individual because He alone is able to see into the hearts of individuals to ensure their repentance is real.

> *offered Himself unblemished by sin to God, cleanse your conscience from dead works and lifeless observances to serve the living God?*
>
> *(Heb. 9:14)*

And it is the cleansing of the inner man, the conscience, from all spiritually dead practices and attractions that is achieved. No longer can the evil one accuse us of being a sinner.

For the Lord in His body and sacrifice has introduced a dramatically new covenant, a new agreement that brings together man and his God

> *For this reason He is the Mediator and Negotiator of the new covenant, by means of death,*
> *(Heb. 9:15a)*

The old arrangement of animal sacrifices did nothing for the conscience and was flawed because of sin and the need to work for salvation by trying to be good and follow the laws and instructions of God.

> *that those who are called may receive the promise of the eternal inheritance.*
> *(Heb. 9:15c)*

The new covenant is based on the death of a perfect man as payment of the condemnation of God against man who sinned, so that those who are called by God may receive the fulfilment of the promised eternal inheritance, which is redemption from the sins committed under the old covenant and an eternity with Him in His glory.

The old covenant was sealed by blood because a will and testament is of no worth without death, and for God to provide a way of salvation that did not require the death of sinful man, a substitute was allowed in the blood of sacrificed calves and goats.

> *In fact under the Law almost everything is cleansed with blood, and without the shedding of blood there is neither forgiveness nor release from sin and its attendant guilt, nor, indeed, the cancellation of the merited punishment for sin.*
> *(Heb. 9:22)*

Even the first covenant did not come into force without the shedding of blood. When Moses read out every commandment of God in the law, he took the blood of sacrificed calves and goats, together with water and scarlet wool and with a bunch of hyssop and sprinkled both the scroll and all the people saying, *"this is the sealing and ratifying blood of the covenant which God commanded me to deliver to you."*

It was necessary for the earthly copies of the heavenly things to be cleansed by this means, but the heavenly things themselves required far better sacrifices than these.
(Heb. 9:23)

This is the difference between the two covenants. For the ratification of the first covenant the blood of animals was used. But for this final covenant a far more appropriate means was required. The blood of a perfect man, a man who could only have come from the purity of heaven in the form of the Son of God, a member of the trinity who willingly allowed Himself to subjected to the mistreatment of men and be killed and to spill His own blood and then to rise up from death to demonstrate that death was not the end but merely a process of proceeding from one life to another.

For Christ did not enter into a holy place made with hands, a mere copy of the true one,
(Heb. 9:24)

When Moses was called upon to make a tabernacle it was to be an exact copy of the tabernacle he saw in heaven, for which he received the plans. It was to be the home of God on the earth, even though Solomon admitted God was far too expansive to be able to fit into it, but it represented His dwelling place.

But the Son did not enter the physical temple in Jerusalem built by Herod, for that was corrupted by the curtain separating the holy place in which priests regularly attended to the golden candelabra (Menorah), the table of shewbread and the altar of incense, and the Holy of Holies in which the high priest alone entered on the day of atonement being torn in two from top to bottom, instead:

He entered into heaven itself, now to appear in the very presence of God on our behalf;
(Heb. 9:24)

Whereas the Aaronic high priests had to continually sacrifice animals whenever they entered into the earthly tabernacle; the Lord was the once for all sacrifice.

Just as it is appointed for all men to die once and after this comes certain judgment, (see 2 Peter 3:10 - 13)

When God created Adam and placed him on the earth, this was to be his testing ground regarding his loyalty to the God who created him. He failed in that test. But because of its fixed size and the command of God for man to multiply and fill the earth it was clear that there would come a time when the multitude of mankind grew so large that the earth could not contain them. So God put a time limit on the life of the earth.

But where was man to go at the end of the world and when the whole of creation burned up in a mighty fire ball?

God lives in endless space. Just as He created the earth and its surrounding cosmos, He was also able to create an eternal home for man in which man would not marry and have children but be as the angels.

Because of sin, however, God also created a place where those who had rejected Him, ignored Him or fought against Him would be put. For eternity. A place completely devoid of His presence.

For Christ, having offered Himself up once for sin, was reinstated with His Father and the Spirit in His place of rest.

So Christ, having been offered once and once for all to bear the burden of the sins of many,

As a perfect Man He was the all sufficient sacrifice for the sins of many. But, according to the prophetic word, He will

return to the earth and appear a second time but in glory not to deal with sin, and to bring the call to come to Him to those who are eagerly and confidently waiting for Him.
(Heb. 9:28)

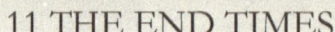

11 THE END TIMES

The world will come to an end and be a thing of the past. As the Lord said, *"Heaven and earth will pass away but my words will never pass away."*

> *For I assure you, until heaven and earth pass away, not the smallest letter or stroke will pass from the Law until all things are accomplished. (Matt. 5:8, 24:35; Lk. 21:33, 16:17; Rev. 2:1, 20:11)*

In the previous chapter we considered all that befell the Messiah in His bid to provide the antidote to sin, by Himself dying on the cross and rising again. As Paul wrote to the Corinthians:

> *But now Christ is risen from the dead,*
> *and has become the firstfruits*
> *of those who have fallen asleep.*
> *(1 Cor. 15:20)*

This ties in with what he wrote to the Thessalonians:

> *But I do not want you to be ignorant, brethren, concerning those who have fallen asleep, lest you sorrow as do others who have no hope.*
> *For if we believe that Jesus died and rose again, even so God will bring with Him those who sleep in Jesus.*

(1 Thes. 4:13, 14)

Jesus rose again from the dead so that death is not the end but the beginning of a new life both here and in the future

> *For this we say to you by the word of the Lord, that we who are alive and remain until the coming of the Lord will by no means precede those who are asleep.*
> *(1 Thes. 4:15)*

Continuing the theme of those who have 'fallen asleep in the Lord', that is those believers who have died having faith in the Lord Jesus Christ are not dead but asleep in the Lord until His second coming when they will arise from their sleep before we who are left are called to be with the Lord.

> *For the Lord Himself will descend from heaven with a shout, with the voice of an archangel, and with the trumpet of God.*
> *(1 Thes. 4:16)*

The second coming of the Lord Jesus will not be a quiet affair as was His first appearance as the Messiah, but with a great cacophony of sound. First the voice of an archangel followed by the trumpet, the great shofar, of God and then the appearance of the Lord along with those that have died in the Lord.

> *And the dead in Christ will rise first.*
> *Then we who are alive and remain shall be caught up together with them in the clouds to meet the Lord in the air. And thus we shall always be with the Lord. Therefore comfort one another with these words.*
> *(1 Thes. 4:16, 17)*

The Day of the Lord

In Joel 1:15 and Amos 5:18 the day of the Lord is mentioned:

> *15 Alas for the day!*
> *For the day of the Lord is at hand;*
> *It shall come as destruction from the Almighty.*

(Joel 1:15)

Woe to you who desire the day of the Lord!
For what good is the day of the Lord to you?
It will be darkness, and not light.
(Amos 5:18)

In Joel the day of the Lord can mean a number of things. It can refer to an extraordinary event such as a plague of locusts (2:1, 11), which in this case referred to the coming of the Assyrian army to subjugate the nation, or an event in the near future such as the destruction of Jerusalem or the defeat of enemy nations, or the final period of history when God will defeat all the forces of evil.

Even when referring to a present event, the day of the Lord inevitably foreshadows the final day of the Lord which has two aspects to it. The last judgement on all evil and sin, and in contrast the final reward for faithful believers. Righteousness will prevail, but not before much suffering (Zech. 14:1 – 3).

28 "And it shall come to pass afterward
That I will pour out My Spirit on all flesh;
Your sons and your daughters shall prophesy,
Your old men shall dream dreams,
Your young men shall see visions.
29 And also on My menservants and on My maidservants
I will pour out My Spirit in those days.
30 "And I will show wonders in the heavens and in the earth:
Blood and fire and pillars of smoke.
31 The sun shall be turned into darkness,
And the moon into blood,
Before the coming of the great and awesome day of the Lord.
32 And it shall come to pass
That whoever calls on the name of the Lord
Shall be saved.
For in Mount Zion and in Jerusalem there shall be deliverance,
As the Lord has said,
Among the remnant whom the Lord calls.
(Joel 2)

Verse 28 was quoted by Peter on the day of Pentecost. Here Joel, after the invasion and deliverance of Israel from the northern army is raising their minds to expect extraordinary spiritual blessings which constitute the true restoration of God's people (Is. 44:3).

This was fulfilled on the day of Pentecost amongst the Jews with a spin off involving Gentiles such as the household of the centurion Cornelius. The oppression of the church by the Jewish religious authorities caused its dispersion throughout the Roman empire and beyond, with the Jews becoming the seedsmen of the elected church, as the preachers (sower of the seed) of the new Word of God.

The church, as founded by the Lord Jesus Christ, was gathered out of the Jews initially but quickly infected Gentiles, so they will become the harvestmen of the church worldwide which will be set up at the coming of the Messiah.

The promise was not restricted to the first Pentecost as Peter said,

> *For the promise is to you and to your children,*
> *and to all who are afar off,*
> *as many as the Lord our God will call."*
> *(Acts 2:39)*

What is written is not about restricted 'drops' as in the First Testament days for as John wrote:

> *He who believes in Me, as the Scripture has said, out of his heart*
> *will flow rivers of living water." But this He spoke concerning the*
> *Spirit, whom those believing in Him would receive; however the*
> *Holy Spirit was not yet given, because Jesus was not yet glorified.*
> *(Jn. 7:38, 39)*

What is also clear Joel's prophecy was in relation to all flesh, not the restricted few as in the First Testament days:

> *That I will pour out My Spirit on **all flesh**;*
> *Your sons and your daughters shall prophesy,*
> *Your old men shall dream dreams,*
> *Your young men shall see visions.*
> *(Joel 2:28)*

That did not mean Israel was no longer God's first born son, rather that the Holy Spirit would have a greater influence over all mankind in order to shame Israel, making them jealous and spur them into fully engaging with Him, which has happened and is happening today.. The criteria for the Holy Spirit to fully come into a person to influence them has remained the same. Repentance and the total commitment to Christ by the repentant sinner.

Although in the days of the First Testament it was limited to those fully engaged in the Lord's work as prophets or men of God who were discerning. In the Second Testament days and beyond the Holy Spirit was available to **all flesh**, whatever your station in life might be.

In emphasis Joel was led to write, *And it shall come to pass that whoever calls on the name of the Lord shall be saved*, for salvation has always been for all men of all nations, not just the Jewish priests or ordinary Jews.

It must be emphasized that Jesus is to be our example in commitment for as Paul wrote to the Philippians:

> *Let this mind be in you which was also in Christ Jesus, who, being in the form of God, did not consider it robbery to be equal with God, (Phil. 2:5)*

Jesus was God, an intrinsic part of God, a full member of the divine trinity with all the power and authority that goes with that position. After all it was He who spoke the words of the Father for the Spirit of God to create the complex world and cosmos.

The current fear of astronomers that something from outer space will hit the earth is miss founded because God will not allow anything to happen to the earth that is not in His will for it to happen. And He it is who created the earth and everything in it, and He it is who is in total control of the heavens and the earth, for it is in His power to *shake the heavens and the earth, the sea and the dry land.*

Even though Jesus was God yet for our sakes:

> *He made Himself of no reputation, taking the form of a bondservant, and coming in the likeness of men. And being found in appearance as a man, He humbled Himself and became obedient to*

the point of death, even the death of the cross. (Phil. 2:7, 8)

This was a low ebb for the one who was to be King of kings and Lord of Lords, the pits, being pushed around by those He had been part of creating, being abused in three illegal trials with false witnesses telling lies and the judge and jury baying for His blood.

With His body being whipped and made bloody by thongs with pieces of bones inserted into them, being crowned with a crown of thorns tearing into the skin of His scalp. And then being made to carry His own cross for execution before someone, a stranger, being forced to carry it for Him. Then being nailed on that cross in a contorted manner and suffering enormous pain before releasing His Spirit for His battered body to die.

It is this humility, although not in every case to the same extent of suffering, that is required of all those that believe in Him, from the least to the greatest. We are all on a journey through life. We are all being tested as to our commitment to Him. It is our willingness to put ourselves second to His will and purpose for us that is key to our success in His service.

> *Therefore God also has highly exalted Him and given Him the name which is above every name, that at the name of Jesus every knee should bow, of those in heaven, and of those on earth, and of those under the earth, and that every tongue should confess that Jesus Christ is Lord, to the glory of God the Father (Phil. 2:9 – 11).*

No wonder the Father exalted Him and gave him a name that is above every name, for He is without doubt our example. No wonder we bow the knee to Him who came for ultimate glory to the earth and suffered great mental, physical and psychological pain and discomfort in being treated abominably by those who should have been in awe of Him and accepted Him for what and who He was.

But it was because of His willingness to go through that trauma, that abuse and suffer as He did that we are saved to the uttermost. That we can look to the future with joy in our hearts.

It is true that Jesus is part of God, but God is three in One, and there is a hierarchy within the Godhead. The Father is the senior which we know because, *"No one knows, however, when that day, the day of the Lord's return, and hour will come. Neither the angels in heaven nor the Son; for only the Father knows.* The Spirit of God is the one who carries out the instructions of the Father as He receives it through the word of the Son.

But the end will come when *Christ will overcome all spiritual rulers, authorities, and powers, and will hand over the Kingdom to God the Father.* Then as a dutiful Son, when *all things have been placed under Christ's rule, then he himself, the Son, will place himself under God, who placed all things under him; and God will rule completely over all.*

In the meantime we *must be patient. Keep your hopes high, for the day of the Lord's coming is near.*

For He will come for:

> *7Behold, He is coming with clouds, and every eye will see Him, even they who pierced Him. And all the tribes of the earth will mourn because of Him. Even so, Amen.*
> *8"I am the Alpha and the Omega, the Beginning and the End,"* says the Lord, *"who is and who was and who is to come, the Almighty."*
>
> (Rev. 1:7, 8)

ABOUT THE AUTHOR

After an electrical engineering apprenticeship in the Royal Navy, Peter went on to serve on a number of ships in different parts of the world, finally being responsible for the weapons maintenance department of a frigate and lecturing to trainee officers on weapon control systems. He also spent two years at the Royal Navy's training college in Fareham, Hampshire instructing on underwater weapon and defense systems.

Leaving the service in 1969, Peter worked as a quality engineer for the British Aircraft Corporation on spacecraft and guided weapon systems before moving to R. A Lister (Diesels) where he became a technical author in 1984. He then worked as a contract author, mostly in the nuclear generation industry, writing operating instructions, maintenance manuals and other instructional and training documentation before finally retiring in 2011. Peter gained membership of the Society of Authors in 1993

For over 20 years, Peter was a Methodist Local Preacher before becoming an official prison visitor and worshipping with his wife at the prison he visited in order to focus on supporting prisoners who wanted to change their lives around. He resigned as a prison visitor in January 2016 after 26 years but continued to attend worship services at the prison chapel for four more years.

Peter met a Jew named Derek who had become a Christian in prison. On his release to the local community, Peter was able to help him adjust to a new life of going straight.

It was Derek who first asked Peter to write on scripture. After which Derek's brother Aaron, a rabbi serving in the USA, came under the influence of Peter's writing and became a Christian. Aaron asked him to write first on the book of Revelation and then on the subject of Moses' Tent of the Meeting, which he self-published early 2011. He currently has 18 books available through Amazon worldwide as a paperback or for downloading to an eBook reader.

Peter has been married for 57 years (December 2018) with three sons and six grandchildren. His autobiographical book explaining how he came to write so many books is called "A Tale of Three Men".

www.ingramcontent.com/pod-product-compliance
Lightning Source LLC
Chambersburg PA
CBHW021119130626
46554CB00002B/774